W9-CKM-246

Muhammad

# ALI

THE GREATEST

EVERLAST
EVERLA

# Muhammad ALI

## THE GREATEST

John Hennessey

PRC

This edition first published in 1999 by
PRC Publishing Ltd,
Kiln House, 210 New Kings Road, London SW6 4NZ

© 1999 PRC Publishing Ltd

All rights reserved. No part of this publication may
be reproduced, stored in a retrieval system, or transmitted
in any form or by any means, electronic, mechanical,
photocopying, recording, or otherwise, without the prior
written permission of the Publisher and copyright holders.

ISBN 1 85648 542 0

Printed and bound in China

# CONTENTS

Previous page: A poet and a pounder — The Greatest in 1966.

Right: c. 1963, Cassius Clay kisses his mother near his father and brother at the Carlerton Hotel.

From the time he beat Polish veteran Zbigniew Piertrzkowski to win the 1960 Olympic light-heavyweight gold medal in Rome, Ali, then known as Cassius Clay, was destined for the top, destined to be something extra special. Though his involvement with Black Power leader Malcolm X and the Muslim faith caused him untold troubles in his early professional life, and his refusal to accept conscription for Vietnam almost cost him his career, Ali remained true to his beliefs and was, in time, recognized as the world's best-known man. Better known, perhaps, than the Pope or any American President! His 'Float like a Butterfly, Sting like a Bee' motto, inspired by faithful handler Bundini Brown, became a worldwide catch phrase, as did his 'I am The Greatest, I am The Prettiest' exhortations before, during and after his colorful boxing contests.

Derided as a frightened clown before his first world heavyweight challenge against the then awesome Sonny Liston, Cassius Clay appeared deranged at the weigh-in and doctors were alarmed at his blood pressure. An hour later, having laughed his head off behind the scenes, he was resting peacefully, his pulse back to normal. That night, 25 February 1964, Clay bamboozled nearly every boxing critic and expert by forcing a bewildered Liston to quit on his stool, supposedly with torn shoulder muscles, at the end of the sixth round. Clay, the perfectly proportioned new heavyweight titleholder, the second youngest in history behind Floyd Patterson, was to become Muhammad Ali, the black people's champion. And, even before the obligatory return match with Liston, the legend had begun. For the next decade and a half, apart from three-and-a-half barren years when he was counted out by the authorities, Ali thrilled millions around the world with his unbelievable multi-punch combinations and Fred Astaire footwork.

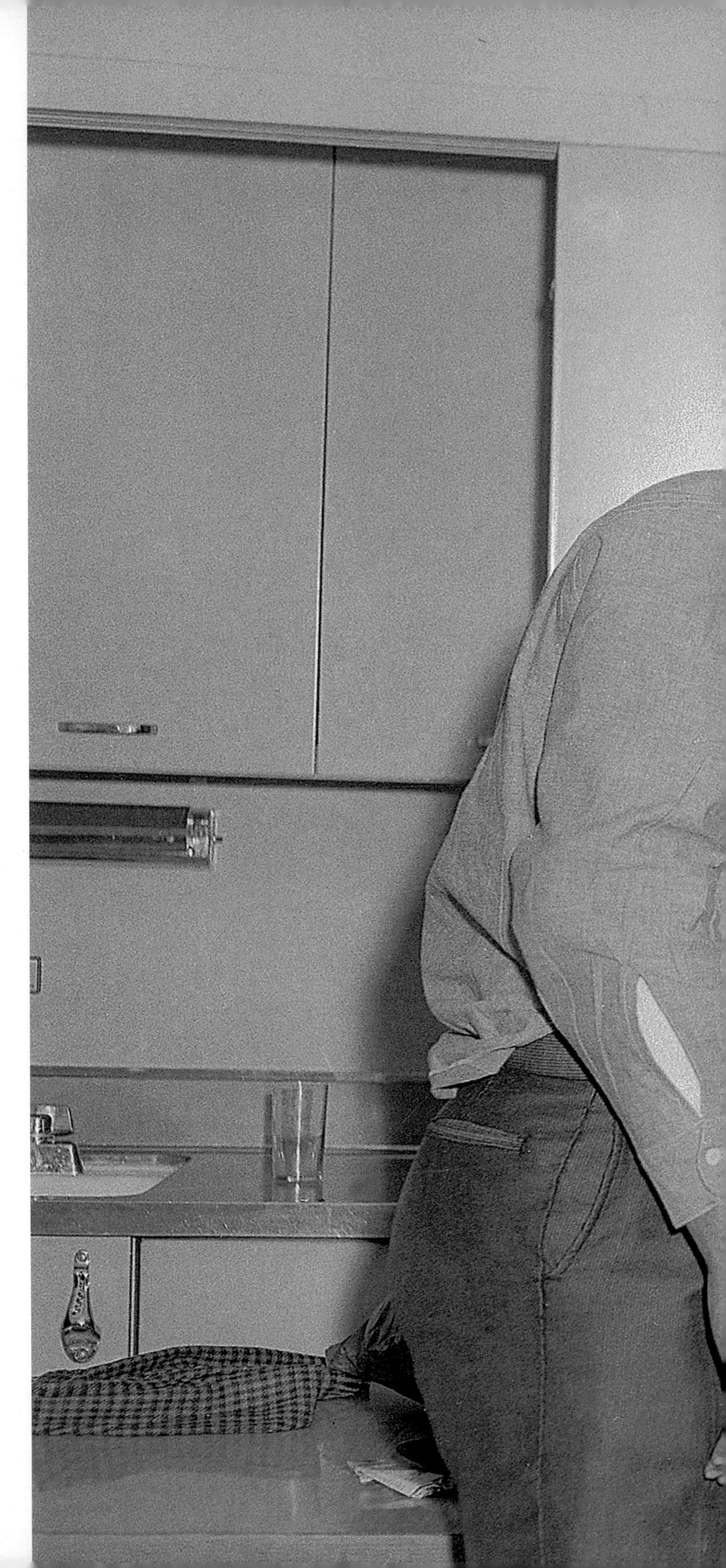

**Right: 'London here I come.' Clay announces his fight with Britain's Brian London. . . in London. It was one of his easisi-est defenses.**

**Far Right: 3 May, 1964. Posing for the cameras in New York City.**

Today, George Foreman says: 'Ali's the one who made it possible for us to earn such huge purses. To call him the greatest boxer of all time doesn't do him justice. He transcended boxing and inspired all athletes. He lifted baseball players, footballers and others, and inspired them to greater things.'

Some hated Ali's brashness but most forgave him because of the beauty he introduced to a brutal sport. Those who loved him wept tears of sadness when he lost for the first time in his career, against Joe Frazier for the undisputed heavyweight crown. They shed even more tears during his comeback when he broke his jaw in the second round against the tough Ken Norton but demonstrated his supreme courage by carrying on to the end only to suffer another defeat. Then came tears of joy when, on one of the most momentous nights in heavyweight history, he destroyed the unbeaten monster George Foreman in what he labeled the 'Rumble in the jungle.' His third Frazier epic, the 'Thrilla in Manila,' overtook the Rumble for nerve-racking, pulse-quickening, raw excitement. Every fight fan marveled at the tenacity and courage of both fighters through 14 of the most ferocious rounds ever staged. Still Ali wouldn't call it a day after his two fiercest battles, and when he took the young Leon Spinks too lightly in 1978 he paid the price with defeat against a novice and we wept tears of incredulity.

Nine months on and slim, trim Ali was restored to the throne after a one-sided revenge points win against Spinks. He slid into retirement. . . and if only he'd stayed there. Having become the first man to

# tomorrow's CHAMPION

HIS TRAINING HAD FINISHED FOR THE DAY AND 14-YEAR-OLD CASSIUS MARCELLUS CLAY BATTLING ON HIS MOTORIZED SCOOTER AGAINST the rain, suddenly heard the roar of a crowd blaring from the radio of a parked car. What happened next almost certainly decided his destiny because he stopped, eager to know what was going on, and heard the announcement over the noise — 'And still heavyweight champion of the world, Rocky Marciano.' The youngster from Louisville, Kentucky, where blacks and whites were still segregated, had already harbored thoughts of becoming a pro boxer. And now, as he continued his journey, his dreams ran away with him — 'And still heavyweight champion of the world, Cassius Clay.'

POST
OU KY

He and Marciano were later to become good pals, but at the time Clay was a skinny kid, and hardly looked like filling out. More of a hurdle was the fact that he couldn't even beat some of the youngsters in his own gymnasium. But such was his desire to succeed that he became obsessed with winning, with being the best in his club to start with, then the best in his age group, and so on. The obsession led him to study in detail all the great fighters on TV and he drew encouragement from each one. Already Clay had discovered his ability to lean away from shots, to entice opponents to throw wasted punches, and he surmised that it was easier to avoid punches like that than to bob from side to side. His unique style, unparalleled in boxing history, was at the formative stage but he loved Sugar Ray Robinson, the fastest fighter in the world who had all the moves and, more especially, a stunning KO punch.

Training came easy to Clay. Because his family was poor, there was seldom enough money for Cassius and his big brother Rudy to take the bus to school each day. So Clay used to race it, pretending in part that he actually wanted to. He also used to measure up against the horses at the local racecourse when they were riding out each day. But even at that early age, despite a strict upbringing by his parents, he had become a boaster and was seen by some as an obnoxious big mouth. His trainer, Joe Martin, even threatened to pull him out of the Olympic trials at the semi-final stage if he didn't stop bragging following local newspaper criticism.

Once he'd achieved a degree of fame he was quickly labeled the 'Louisville Lip' by the Press. By that time it didn't matter though, because he could always be counted on to drum up publicity for his fights.

Ali discovered boxing by accident after his precious new bicycle, a Christmas present from his father, had been stolen. The distraught 12-year-old was told by a passer-by to report the theft to the local policeman, Joe Martin, who also ran the Columbia Gym. The smell of the gym and its surroundings captivated the boy, and after he saw Martin working as a corner man on TV during an amateur boxing show called 'Tomorrow's Champion,' he was hooked.

His first efforts were pitiful because he had no technique and, surprisingly, appeared to have little natural talent either. All he could do was thrash away with all his might in the hope that his opponents would succumb. They did. Within weeks, he had fought and won his first bout and inside a year he, too, was appearing on TV. Yet all he had to offer was raw courage until defeat by a classier opponent in the 'Golden Gloves' competition opened his eyes to the skill necessary to survive. Soon he was frequenting Fred Stoner's gym on the other side of town where his conqueror trained, much against Martin's wishes, and Ali insists he learned the finer points of the sport there. Stoner told him: 'You got the will but you don't have the skill.' That was to follow, rapidly, and Ali says in his colorful 1975 autobiography *The Greatest*: 'All the publicity about my boxing origins and the early development describes Joe Martin as the incubator. But my style, my stamina, my system were molded down in the basement of a church in East End, where Stoner ran his club.' At this early stage of his career, Clay was winning considerable support in his home town from frequent TV excursions, and he stirred up even more interest by promising to 'whip' his next opponent. 'I'd mouth off to anyone who'd listen about what I was going to do to anyone who fought me,' he recalled. 'I was only a kid fighter yet I was a drawing card because people would tune in hoping to see me beat.' His opponents were unlucky!

Once he'd developed his style there was no stopping him and his rise to fame in the amateur ranks, from lightweight through the divisions, was rapid. His

**Previous Page: At 12-years-old Cassius Clay shows his best pugilist stance.**

**Left: 6 February, 1962. Cassius Clay, the Louisville slugger, a handsome 20-year-old, had been fighting since 29 October, 1960, and had won all of his ten fights — seven by knockout.**

Left: 1 September, 1960, Rome, Italy. Cassius Clay jolts Russian boxer Shatkov with a right to the head in their bout.

progress towards the Olympic team was inevitable after he had collected several state titles and the 1959 National 'Golden Gloves' and Amateur Athletic Union titles. Clay repeated the double in 1960. He truly was a golden boy with a glittering future. The AAU crown guaranteed him entry to the Olympic trials in San Francisco and at the tender age of 18 he was America's most experienced competitor. That didn't make him the most popular, though, because of his loud-mouth ways, but he smoothed his path to the final with a succession of victories.

Standing in his way of a place in the Rome Olympics was Army champion Allen Hudson, a vicious puncher who served notice of his intentions by decking Clay with a left hook in the first round. Clay held his own in the second round and in the third and final round, with the fight and his Olympic dream slipping away, the youngster suddenly found an opening. A right cross landed flush on Hudson's jaw and Clay followed up with a dazzling combination which was to become a trademark in the years to follow. The referee stopped the fight, despite Hudson's repeated protests, and Clay was on his way to Rome as the top amateur light-heavyweight in America.

Although Clay insists his main ring education came courtesy of Fred Roper, Martin was his corner man and both trainers were convinced he would win a gold medal. Martin was unable to accompany him to Rome, however, because of a family illness and so the bragging began in earnest again. With no one to calm him down, Clay quickly made himself unpopular in the Olympic village. His outlandish behavior attracted the bulk of media attention, which meant his team-mates were largely overshadowed.

But once again he served up the goods, stopping a Belgian, then outpointing a vastly-experienced Russian in his opening contests. Next on his list was Tony Madigan, the Australian who had inflicted on Clay his

**Right: In typical style, Clay sets himself apart from the rest of the Olympic team.**

first defeat in the 'Golden Gloves.' This time Clay, his confidence sky-high, outsmarted him in a tough contest to reach the final. For all his boasting, Clay really was a polished performer and he proved it again in the final against Piertrzkowski when he battered the Polish champion in a spectacular third round to take the gold. 'I told you I am the greatest,' bellowed the brash youngster, proudly displaying his victor's medal around his neck.

Clay was given a hero's reception when he returned to Louisville and he was in big demand. An Olympic gold was, and still is, the best possible currency for a passport into the pro game and the big time. Martin had lined up a local millionaire businessman to be his manager but Cassius Clay Snr. didn't like the idea and his son was eventually handled by a wealthy 10-man Louisville consortium. They put up a $10,000 signing-on fee — a fortune for the Clay family — and were in return guaranteed 50 percent of his prize money for the six-year contract. It was to prove a magnificent financial investment.

Cassius Clay's entry into the professional ranks was an inauspicious affair. With Fred Stoner in the corner at his request, he plodded through a dreary six-round points win against unknown, unsung Tunny Husaker, a white nohoper heavyweight from Fayetteville in West Virginia. Clay displayed none of the punching power that had made him such a big hit in the Olympics and though he should have been pumped up to the limit on his pro debut, he seemed distinctly uninterested in the affair. The sponsoring group was not impressed, either with Clay or his trainer, and the youngster was soon dispatched to Archie Moore's training camp on the West Coast. Bill Faversham, who headed the group, felt the great old veteran could teach Clay the tricks of the trade because, despite his repertoire of skills, he was, basically, still a novice.

USA
USA

**Right: In 1960, Clay was bigger and so was his reputation.**

Clay, in fact, had already singled out Joe Louis to manage him — but the former heavyweight champion didn't like the young braggart. He also went for Sugar Ray Robinson, who had been a great source of inspiration to the youngster with his own quicksilver skills. Robinson, at the veteran stage of his fighting career, loved the flashy moves Clay demonstrated in front of him but felt it was too early to get involved, a decision he was later to regret. Then came the reunion which was to forge boxing's greatest partnership. Clay, fed up with the dull routines laid down at Moore's San Diego training camp, soon returned to Louisville and met with Angelo Dundee, former manager-coach of world light-middleweight champion Willie Pastrano. Dundee had an impeccable pedigree and the two men remembered each other well.

A few years earlier, a teenage Clay had pestered Dundee for an audience with then contender Pastrano, who was in Louisville for a fight. Clay angled his way up to their hotel bedroom then later sparred a round with him and wanted more, only for Dundee to call a halt.

Angelo undoubtedly liked what he saw, enjoyed the kid's style and loved his enthusiasm. Every time he turned up in Louisville with a fighter, there was Cassius, his brother Rudy and even his mum and dad to greet him. Soon Clay was getting free tickets for the fights. So there was an initial, mutual friendship upon which the two men could build when the subject of training Clay came up. Dundee's friends thought he was crazy to handle the youngster, who just couldn't stop talking about himself But Dundee understood Clay, understood what he was all about and wasn't surprised when the boy insisted on joining him in Miami Beach to prepare for a fight rather than be with the family for Christmas.

Clay settled into a routine at Dundee's gym, but he hated the fact that he couldn't box all the time. The wily Dundee was soon able to utilize the boy's strengths and weaknesses. Clay had to be the instigator, the initiator of all things. Of course, he wasn't, but Dundee allowed him to think he was. 'You can't improve on a fighter's natural ability,' he was to say. 'All I did was improve what he had and add a few wrinkles.' In other words, he allowed Clay to take all the credit for any adjustments that were made to his technique. It wasn't the done thing and it probably wasn't professional to act in this way, but Dundee knew Clay was something special and he was more than happy to improvise. Clay's first fight under Dundee came two days after Christmas at Miami Beach when he met Herb Siler on the undercard of a Willie Pastrano show. Clay KO'd him in four rounds and promptly bragged: 'I'm gonna be the heavyweight champion of the world.' It was to be a familiar message trumpeted after every victory from then on. His next two fights also ended in quick time, then the experienced Donnie Fleeman took him seven rounds before being stopped on cuts. Fleeman had won 45 of his 51 contests and was just the sort of opponent to push Clay. It was new territory for the kid and he handled the situation well. Next came a fight in his hometown, against Lamar Clark, another ring-wise fighter from Utah who boasted a big KO punch. He had seen off 45 opponents in this way but Clay, ever mindful of the publicity and his image, predicted he would sort him out in two rounds. Clay succeeded and, after thrashing his white rival, moved on to Las Vegas for his next bout, against Duke Sabedong. The glamor of the town, and the occasion, got to him, especially when he and Duke were being introduced on local TV. Even as they talked with the interviewer, they were upstaged by the outrageous wrestler 'Gorgeous George,' who had long flowing blond locks and a robe to match. Clay looked on in bewilderment as he took over the show, saying: 'I am the world's

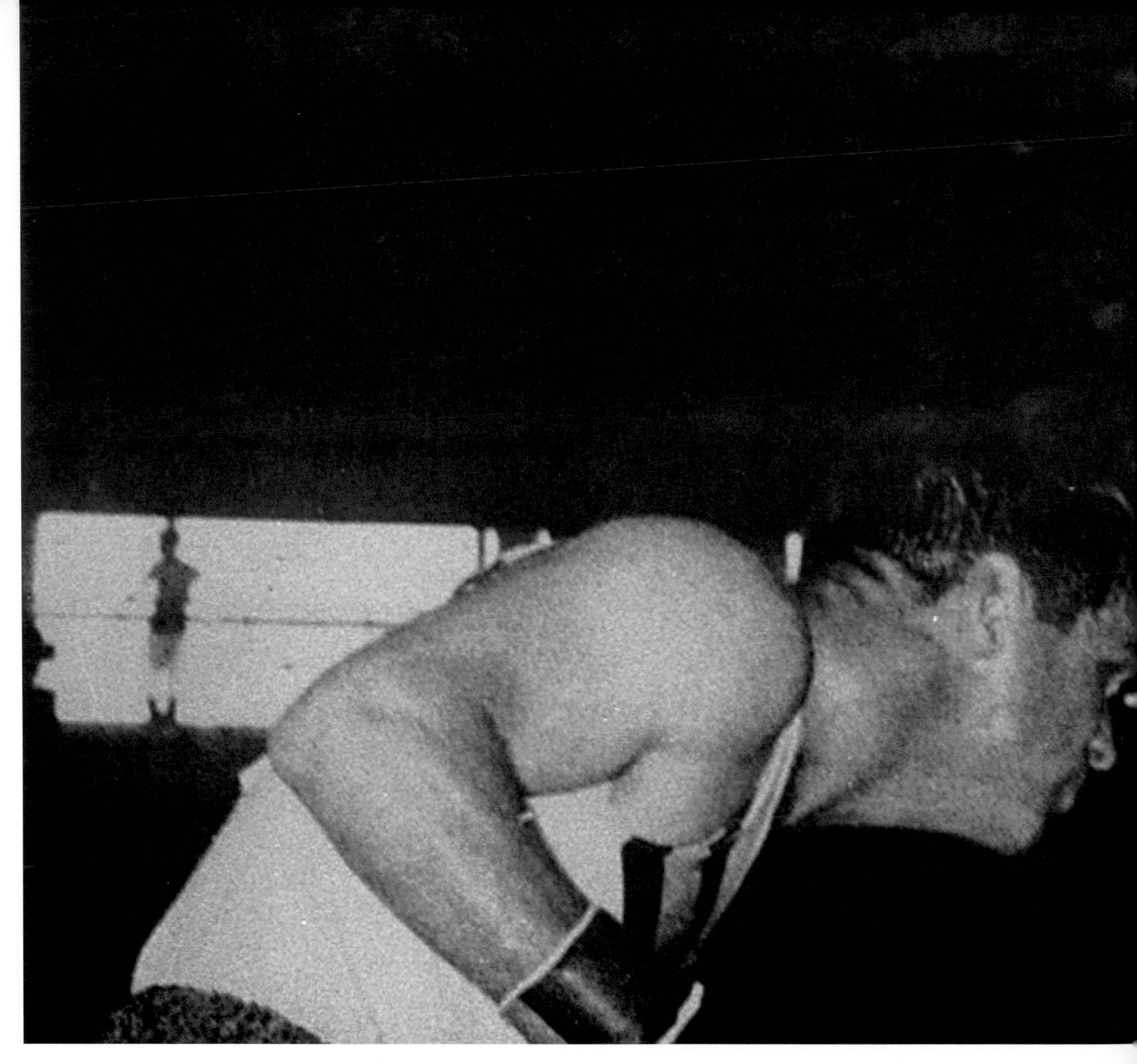

greatest wrestler. I cannot be defeated. I am the greatest. I am the king.'

Clay later recalled the incident, telling reporters that, 'Gorgeous George purred, "look at my velvet skin. Look at my pretty hair. If that bum messes my hair up tomorrow night I'll annihilate him. I want all of you out there to come to the Sports Palace early because I'm gonna mop the floor with this bum. If he beats me I'll cut off my golden hair and throw it out to the audience and go bald.'"

Clay loved the colorful banter and sure enough he was there in the crowd to see Gorgeous George perform the following night. The crowd booed and jeered George, threw paper cups at him and derided him. But he won, as he always did. Just as Clay knew he, too, was destined to be a winner.

Left: 3 September, 1960, Rome, Italy. Cassius Clay throws a hard right at Australia's A. Madigan, during their light-heavyweight semi-final of the Olympic boxing tournament.

The seeds of greatness had been sown before then in Clay's own mind and the Gorgeous act was yet another factor he employed for recognition. Surprisingly, he took 10 laborious rounds to polish off Sabedong, but he was already dreaming of a world title shot. It seemed a ludicrous ambition since Sabedong, while a decent pro, was hardly a springboard for world dreams. But there was no holding him and his next test came against Alonzo Johnson, the first ranked opponent he had fought in his hometown Louisville. Again, Clay was taken the 10-round distance but this time he was much more assured, winning nearly every round and confirming that he was more than prepared to step up into the big time.

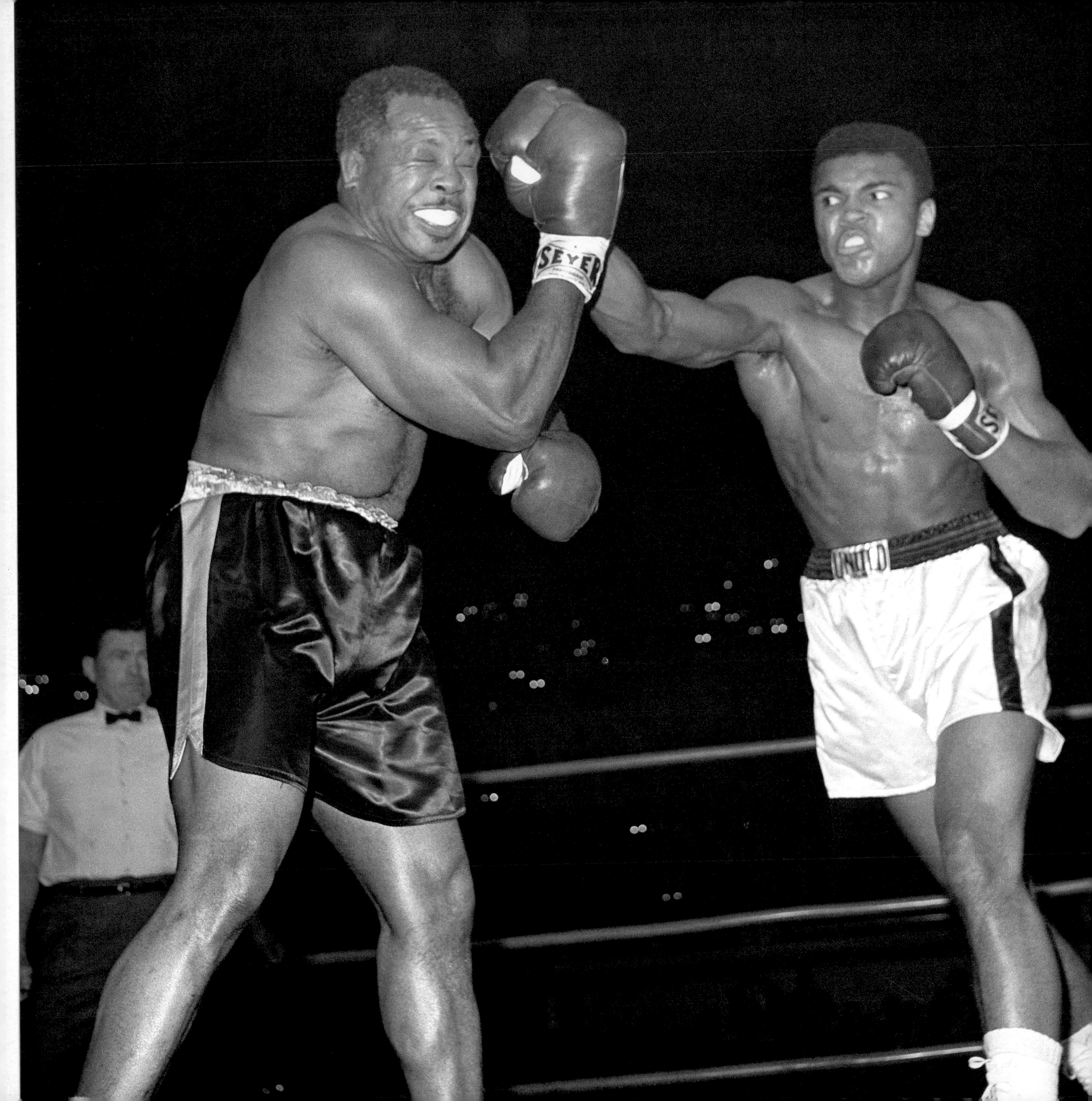

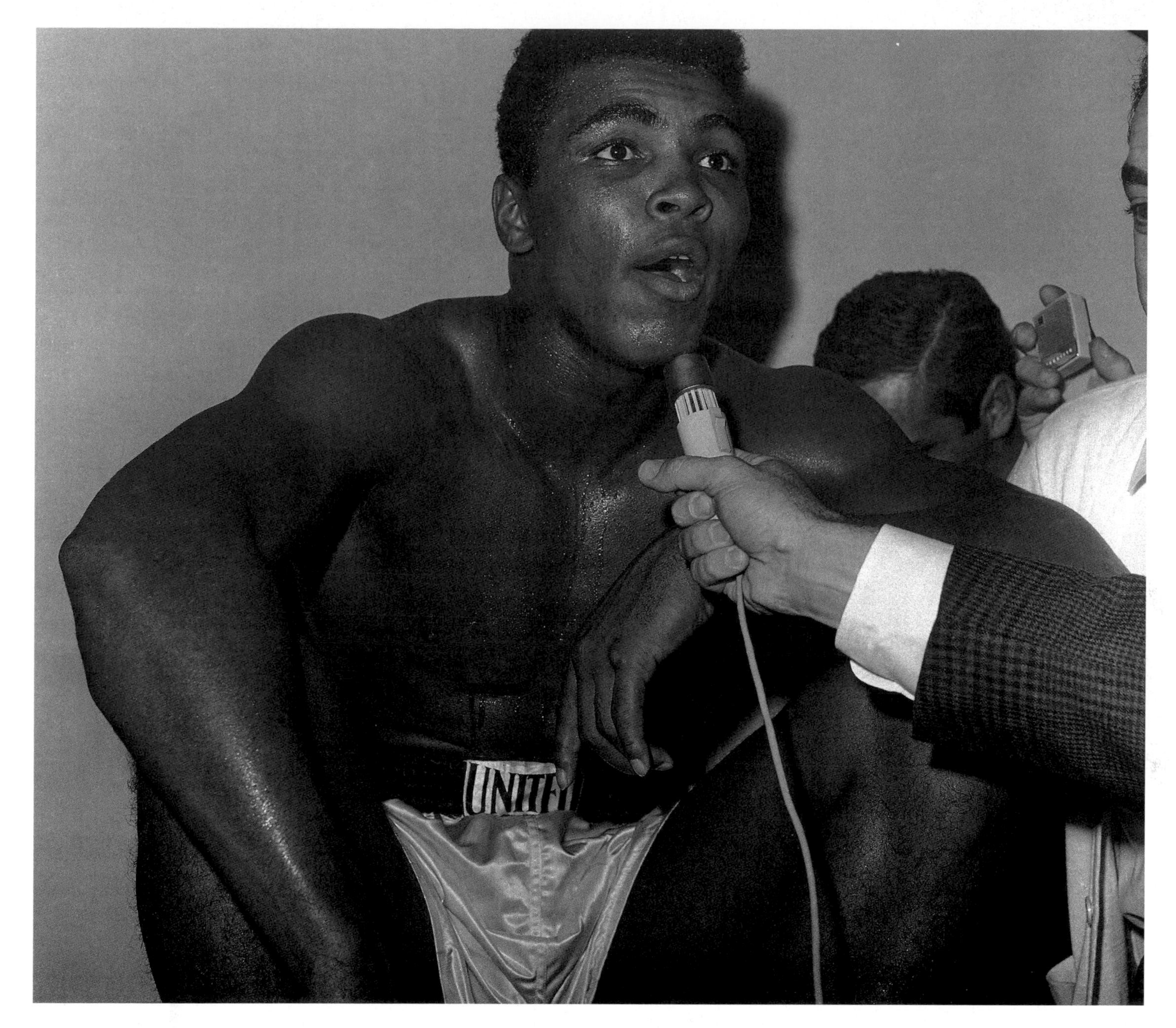


**Previous Page: 28 February, 1962, Miami. Cassius Clay vs. Don Warner. Clay won by a knockout in the 4th round.**

**Left: 16 November, 1962. Cassius Clay talks to newsmen in his dressing room at the Los Angeles Sports Arena late after his heavyweight title elimination bout with Archie Moore. The 20-year-old youth KO'd his 45-year-old opponent in the fourth round as he had said he would.**

**Far Left: 15 November, 1962. Cassius Clay hits Archie Moore with a right to the side of he head in the first round.**

Yet when he did step up a class, with venue and opponent, he very nearly came unstuck because of his cockiness. At short notice, Dundee matched him with another young prospect, Detroit's Sonny Banks, at New York's famed Madison Square Garden, home of American boxing, and Clay couldn't resist predicting: 'The man must fall in the round I call. Banks must fall in four.' It was corny, but the juvenile rhymes attracted even more attention. All eyes were on Clay when he met Banks and for two rounds the script went according to plan as he danced rings around his opponent. But Banks shook him rigid in round three when he caught his clowning opponent with a left hook to the jaw.

He always maintained it was a slip, but either way he recovered his senses to fend Banks off for the

**Right:** 4 March, 1964. The boxer is interviewed by a reporter in front of the United Nations with his brother, Rudolph Valentino Clay, Black Muslim leader Malcolm X, and Nigerian ambassador to the UN S.O. Adebo.

remainder of the round. Then, as if to prove he really hadn't been tagged, Clay came out blazing in the appointed round and carried out his prediction.

Within months Clay had worked himself up to a confrontation with the veteran Archie Moore, whose methods he had shunned when he first turned pro. Moore, a great light-heavyweight champion at his prime, could no longer make the weight and, at 43 years of age — some say much older — this was a final fling for him. Moore reckoned he had developed a 'lip-buttoner' to shut Clay up, but in reality he was no match for the super-slick youngster, who again selected round four with another slushy rhyme that was to be his stock in trade over the years. Sure enough, after coasting through the early stages and flooring him, Clay opened up in the fourth and decked the old-timer again. Moore, still retaining his immense pride, managed to beat the count, but he couldn't beat a champion in the making, and the referee quickly intervened to rescue him. It was November 1962, just 25 months after he had first joined the paid ranks, and for the first time in his 16-fight career, Clay had received national exposure on TV. He had also earned a princely $45,000, his biggest purse, but a mere fraction of what lay ahead. It was the first genuine sign that he had what it took yet, oddly, the win didn't go down well with the fans, who booed him loudly for thrashing the legendary Moore.

Sonny Liston, the giant, brooding heavyweight champion who was at the ringside during the Banks' fight was Clay's next, seemingly improbable target. Though the youngster was now being taken seriously, no one outside his immediate close-knit circle could envisage feeding him to the lion. 'Liston in eight,' bragged a jubilant Clay afterward, but 'Old Stone Face,' as Liston had been dubbed, told Clay chillingly: 'You go eight seconds with me little boy and I'll give you the title.' Most of the media, amused at times by

**Right: c. 1963. Cassius Clay talks on the telephone during his stay at the Carlerton Hotel.**

**Next Page: 13 March, 1963. Pacing the ring after the crowd booed his win in a 1963 bout with Doug Jones.**

Clay's ranting, would love to have seen Liston shut him up once and for all, but they were forced to wait as Clay marked time with a routine three-round win over Charlie Powell, an ex-gridiron footballer. While Liston prepared for a rematch with Floyd Patterson, the hapless world champion he had demolished to win the crown, Clay was being asked by his management for final proof of his credentials with a tough test at the Garden against world number two Doug Jones, who had moved up a division after campaigning for top honors as a light-heavy.

Jones was a Liston lookalike who joined the endless list of exceptional fighters who never managed to win a world title. Jones was tough, like Liston, could even punch like the champion, and he had something extra: unlike Liston, he was a smart fighter. Clay's vanity stopped him from believing anyone could be as smart as him and he underestimated Jones drastically. It almost proved his undoing. His pre-fight rantings failed to unnerve Jones, as they would later do Liston, and his extraordinary speed and skills also failed to ruffle him. Again the youngster predicted round four but Jones was far too good to be suckered and carried the fight to him. Round four came and went and Clay found himself on the receiving end of boos from the crowd. By round five he was being reminded forcefully that he was taking part in a 10-rounder and Jones began cutting back Clay's early lead as the fight went on.

By the ninth there was nothing in it and all that stood between them was guts, sheer guts. And Clay found them as he brought it back up from his boots in two final, stirring rounds to eke out a controversial if correct decision. According to many ringsiders Jones had just sneaked it, but the two judges had Clay winning by a round, while the referee gave it to him comfortably. The braggart had won again but to the sound of boos, yet he'd passed a severe examination of his talent and heart, and was later to demonstrate just how smart he was. As Muhammad Ali, he gave many fighters return matches throughout his career, but Jones was never given that option. Clay wasn't that stupid.

His stock had fallen somewhat with this display, yet Clay was in even bigger demand and, more to the point, a legitimate title challenger. But there was to be one final test before the inevitable showdown with big, bad Liston, who was being hailed as an invincible, cast-iron monster by the Press even before he had destroyed Patterson a second time. Britain's popular Henry Cooper, a cut-prone yet fearsome left-hooker, was the choice and Wembley the venue. For all Clay's bragging about what he would do to the 'tramp,' 'this bum' who would fall in five, many English fans warmed to the handsome American and his daily antics as he trained in Hyde Park. Though they obviously wanted their man to win, Clay proved to be a major attraction, although like many Yanks, there were thousands of Britons who wanted the balding Cooper to shut him up.

Trouble was, victory for Cooper — an improbability given his record — would not have pitched him in with Liston. Cooper's manager, friend and mentor Jim Wicks loved him like a son and had already insisted: 'I wouldn't let Henry in the same town as Liston, let alone the same ring.' Such was the interest that tickets sold out well in advance, but Clay wasn't interested. His mind was focused firmly on Liston, but his lack of respect for Cooper put him on that high-wire again and ultimately provided one of the great talking points of his entire career and an historic moment in British boxing history.

The outrageous Clay arrived at the weigh-in wearing a mock crown and ermine robe proclaiming: 'I'm the next king of boxing' and 'This ain't no jive, Cooper will fall in five.' But 29-year-old Cooper, roared on by

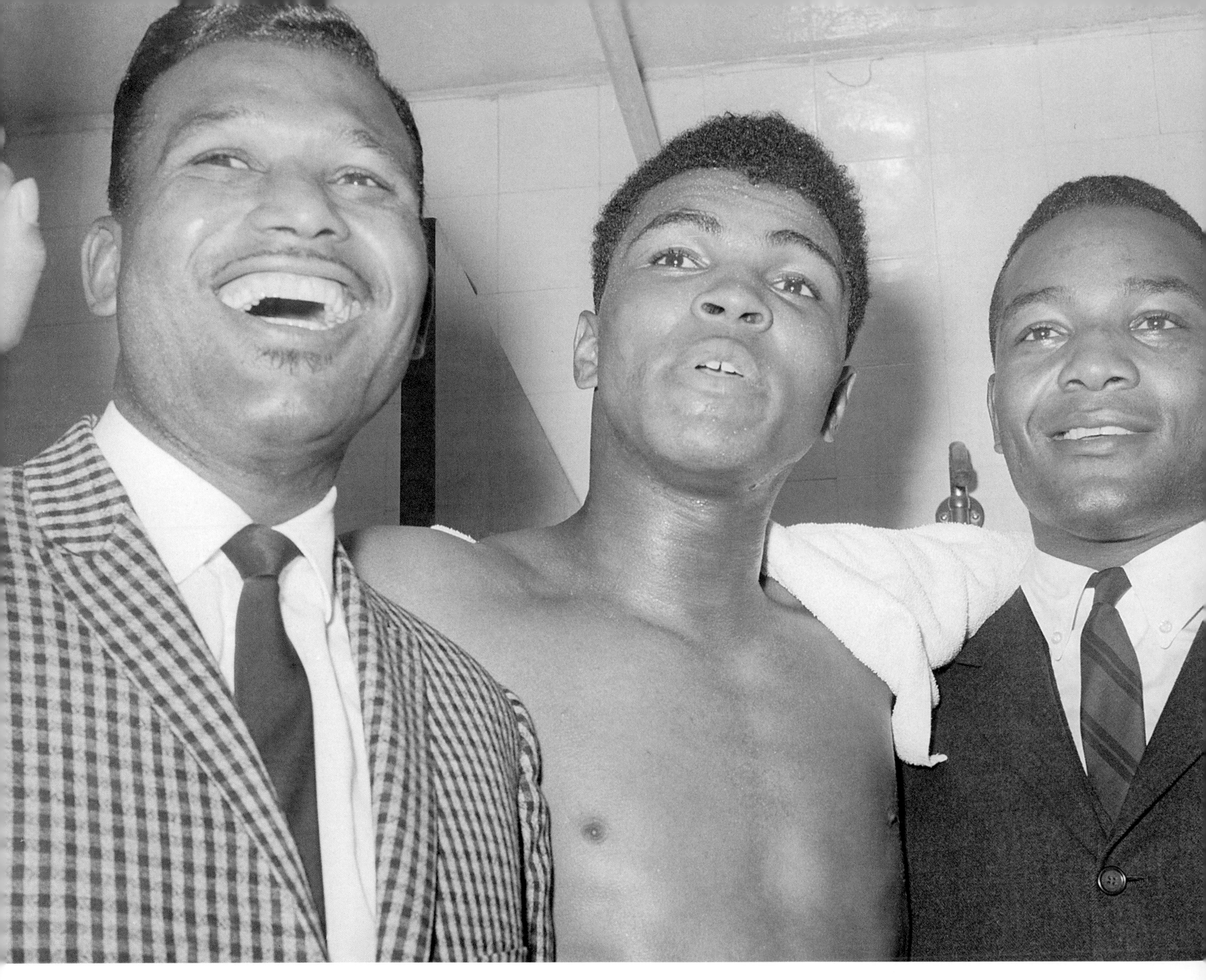

an army of devoted supporters, hadn't read the script. He surprised Clay with an early assault and kept up the pressure throughout round one without causing any real damage. He was relentless, whacking Clay on the break several times, but once the youngster found his range in the next round he began peppering his older opponent with snappy left jabs.

The crowd bayed for Clay's blood but, almost inevitably, what they got was Cooper's as a cut appeared over his left eye. By round three it looked pretty bad and a further cut had materialized over his other eye. The end looked near but Clay, keen to carry

**Left: 18 June, 1963, London, England. Cassius Clay, bewildered by Henry Cooper's unexpected and ferocious opening attack, is pinned on the ropes in the first round of their heavyweight match at Wembley in London. Though Cooper kept up the assault and managed to put Clay down at the end of the fourth round, the American fulfilled his boast and won the fight in the fifth. The referee, Tommy Little, stopped the fight because of cuts over Cooper's eyes.**

**Far Left: 14 March, 1963, New York. A victorious Cassius Clay is joined in his dressing room by Sugar Ray Robinson and Cleveland Browns football star Jimmy Brown. Unbeaten Clay failed to knock out Doug Joes but his long-armed jabs and straight rights did win him an unpopular, unanimous 10-round decision in their heavyweight contenders' fight.**

out his round five prediction, appeared to be coasting when Cooper forced him to the ropes and exploded a magnificent left hook against his jaw. 'Ennry's 'Ammer,' as it was called affectionately, had paid dividends as Clay crumpled against the ropes only to be saved by the bell. 'I was dazed and numb,' he admitted, but to be fair he was looking to his corner for guidance even as he lay on the canvas and we will never know how badly he was hurt. In following years he was to demonstrate his magnificent courage and will to survive time after time, and it is possible he would have been able to hang on and clear his head.

ATTENTION
ALL BOXERS
MUST HAVE BLOODTEST
EXIT

Left: 8 January, 1964, Miami Beach. 'That ape is almost as ugly as Sonny,' says Cassius Clay, as he clowns around with a Ringling Brothers Circus clown dressed in a gorilla costume.

In the event, Dundee was taking no chances. As Clay wobbled back to his corner, his trainer noticed some padding sticking out of his glove. He quickly tore open the glove and insisted on a new pair, thus gaining Clay a valuable minute or so in which to recover. That was all he needed, and with Cooper masked with blood within seconds of the start of round five, referee Tommy Little did the only thing possible under the circumstances and stopped the fight. Even a relieved Clay acknowledged the seriousness of Cooper's condition and showed concern while his new pal Drew Bundini Brown pranced around the ring with the mock crown Clay had worn earlier. 'I'd have knocked him out,' said a disconsolate Cooper, while Clay, viewing the British champion with a new respect, admitted it was the hardest shot he'd ever taken.

Cooper was to be given another chance against his adversary, but on that occasion circumstances were entirely different, even though the outcome was much the same. Cooper, a respected ringside radio commentator today, cemented his claim to Britain's sporting roll of honor in that first encounter, while for Clay it proved to be the last title stepping stone. In the crowd at Wembley was Liston's adviser, Jack Nilon, who must have been convinced a Clay match would be a pushover for his man. 'He wants you,' he told a blood-spattered Clay afterwards. 'He says to drink your orange and your milk shakes and stay healthy. You've talked yourself into a heavyweight fight.' Clay and his handlers were ecstatic. It was time to go hunting.

He was only 21 with just 19 fights behind him, and Clay's pursuit of Liston and his world crown was greeted with a mixture of incredulity and disbelief by most observers. How on earth, they reasoned, could this lippy kid take on the monster who had just driven ex-champion Floyd. Patterson out of town in complete humiliation for the second time? Yet he set

about his task in frenzied fashion, baiting 'The Big Bear' — his own nickname for Liston — at every given opportunity. 'He's too ugly and slow for someone as pretty as me,' screamed Clay as interest mounted throughout the world. Hardly an opponent had failed to be impressed and overawed by Liston, yet Clay derided him, even to the extent of buying a bus which he had painted in several colors. His signwriter father added the inscription 'World's Most Colorful Fighter: Cassius Clay' across one side with 'Liston is great but he'll fall in eight' on the other.

Not content with that, the youngster decided during a promotional crosscountry tour from Los Angeles to New York to call on Liston at his Denver home at 3am. A bemused Liston climbed out of bed to see what was going on and was met with a chorus of shouts from Clay and his pals. Eventually Clay and Co. were moved on by police, but Liston must surely have felt his young opponent was somewhat deranged.

The great Rocky Marciano, the only undefeated world champ in history, certainly thought so. He was convinced Clay was horribly short of experience against a man he classed as a 'brute.' 'It's hard to tell

**Left: 22 January, 1964. The Beatles pose with the World Heavyweight title contender during a visit to one of his training sessions in Miami.**

**Below Left: This is a tale of the tape for the World Heavyweight Championship bout between champion Sonny Liston and contender Cassius Clay.**

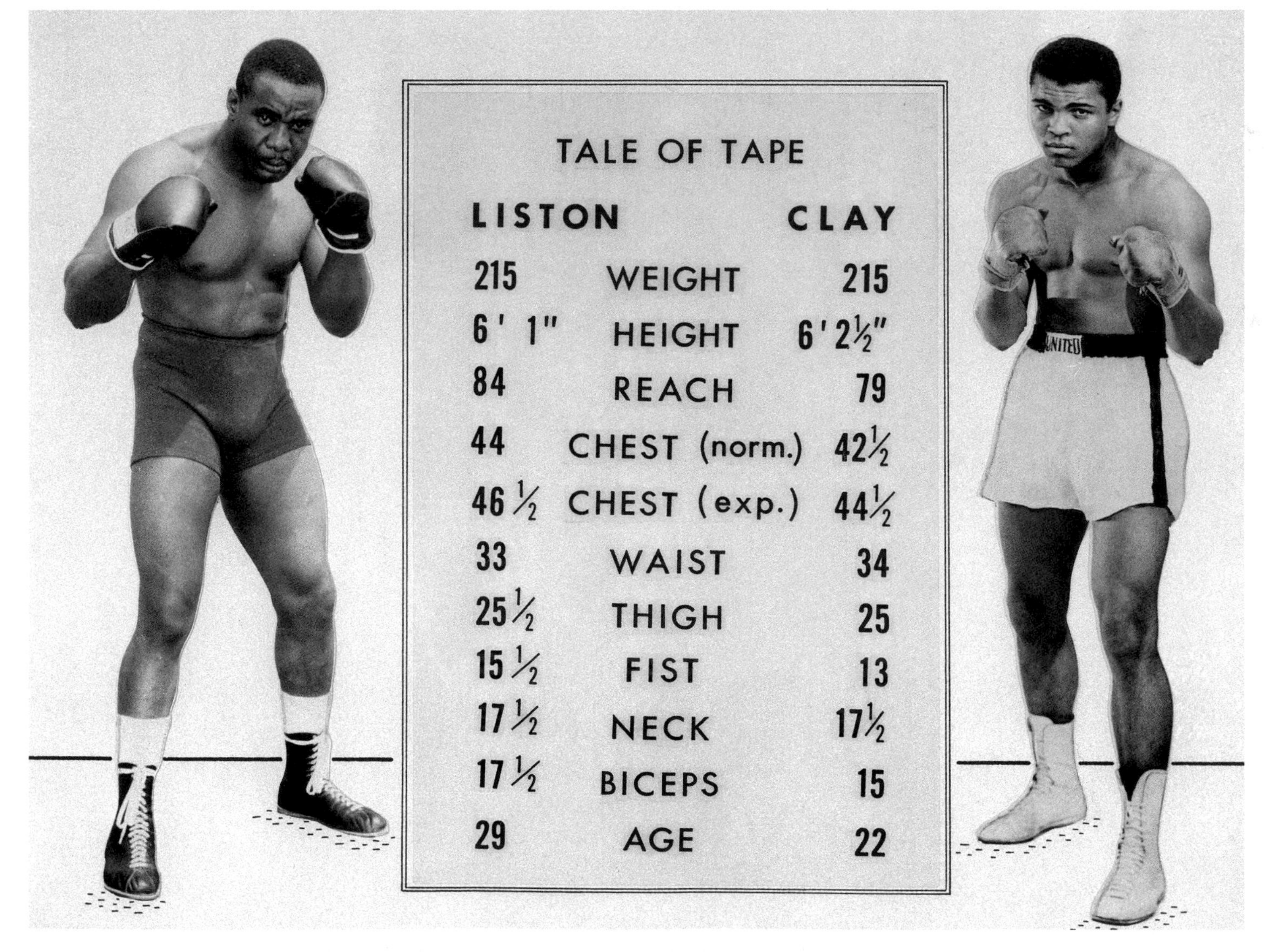

TALE OF TAPE

| LISTON | | CLAY |
|---|---|---|
| 215 | WEIGHT | 215 |
| 6' 1" | HEIGHT | 6'2½" |
| 84 | REACH | 79 |
| 44 | CHEST (norm.) | 42½ |
| 46½ | CHEST (exp.) | 44½ |
| 33 | WAIST | 34 |
| 25½ | THIGH | 25 |
| 15½ | FIST | 13 |
| 17½ | NECK | 17½ |
| 17½ | BICEPS | 15 |
| 29 | AGE | 22 |

Right: 17 December, 1964. Cassius Clay views the body of soul singer Sam Cooke at his wake in Chicago.

Below Right: 6 February, 1964, Miami Beach. Clay listens to trainers Angelo Dundee (Left) and Drew Brown, as he continues his 'psychological warfare' against Sonny Liston.

Far Right: Challenger Cassius Clay strains to break away from a friend who held him as he tried to lunge at champion Sonny Liston during weigh-in ceremonies. Clay was fined $2,500 for his antics by the Miami Beach Boxing Commission.

Clay not to fight this monster now, but I'm sure he'll be more receptive after he's been there with Liston,' said Marciano. Liston, who KO'd Patterson in two minutes ten seconds, referred to Clay as a'fag' and added: 'If they ever make the fight I'll be locked up for murder.' But make it they did with Clay receiving a purse of nearly $500,000, enormous for a challenger but, after all, he was the star attraction.

The two men met face to face for the first time on 5 November, 1963, to sign for the fight. 'He's an old man,' said Clay afterwards. 'I'll give him talking lessons and boxing lessons.' The 'talking lessons' continued throughout the build-up to their 25 February 1964 confrontation in Miami then Clay appeared to flip his lid completely at the weigh-in. With 'Bear Hunting' emblazoned across his denim jacket, he stunned a

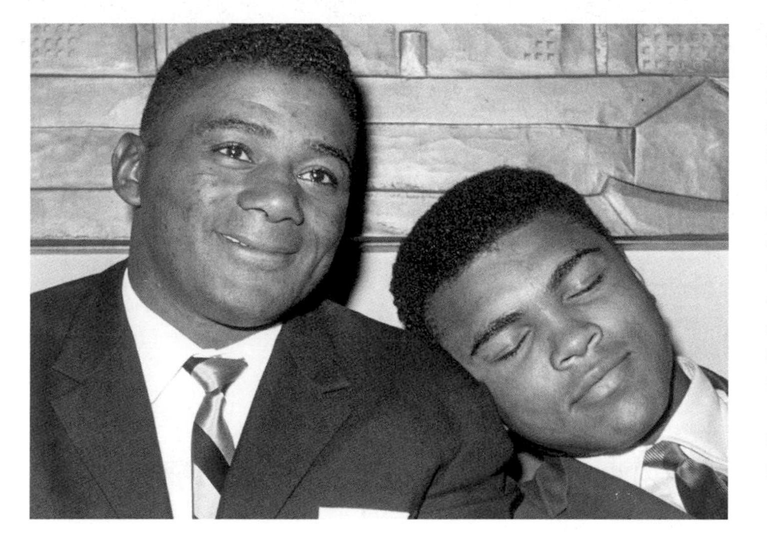

**Far Left: Muhammad Ali continues his verbal attack as he starts through the ropes toward former heavyweight king Floyd Patterson (Right) at the latter's training camp. After a heated argument about names — Patterson insisted on calling the champ 'Cassius Clay' and Clay called Floyd 'rabbit' — Ali challenged Patterson to a bout on the spot. 'Let's do it,' replied Floyd.**

**Left: Best of friends again, Ali relaxes on Patterson's shoulder.**

wasn't able to put him away throughout the one-sided contest.

Three months later Ali, having previously failed his Army induction exam, was reassessed as being fit for duty in Vietnam after the pass mark had been lowered. His response was to say war was against his new beliefs and added: 'I ain't got no quarrel with the Viet Cong. They ain't called me a nigger.' The statement enraged white America and again Ali, now managed by the shrewd Muslim Herbert Muhammad, found himself an outcast. He had been stripped of his title by the World Boxing Association and was due to meet Ernie Terrell, a tall, black fighter who had been put up as the WBA champion. But after virtually every American state refused the fight, Terrell pulled out.

Ali was forced to defend his title on foreign soil — albeit only across the border in Canada — and his new opponent was the rough, tough, clumsy George Chuvalo, who managed to last the full 15 rounds. Two months later, in May 1966, Ali flew to London for a rematch with Henry Cooper at Highbury Stadium, home of Arsenal Football Club. This time there were no dramas. Cooper, bleeding profusely from cuts, was retired inside six rounds without ever looking capable of knocking over his young rival again. By now the British public and Press had taken Ali to their hearts

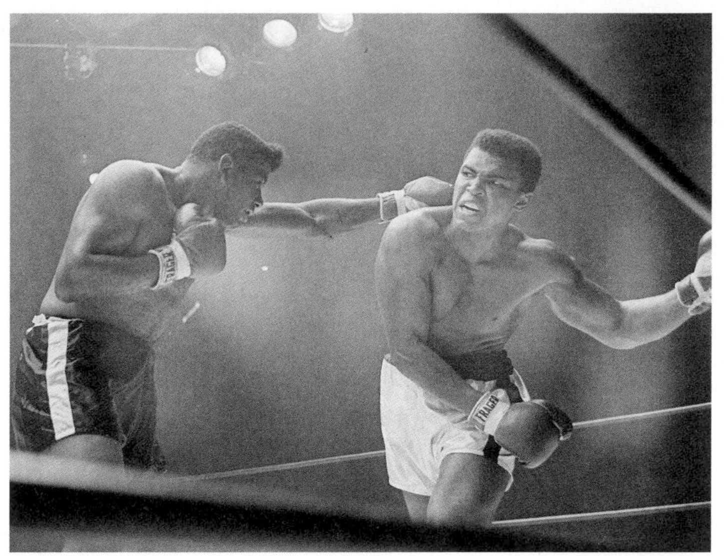

**Left: 22 November, 1965, Las Vegas. A snarling Muhammad Ali ducks under a long left jab by former champion Floyd Patterson, in the Las Vegas Convention Center during the sixth round of their scheduled 15-round title bout. Clay bounced back to deck the 30-year-old Patterson later in the round for a mandatory eight count.**

**Far Left: Ali dances away from contender Floyd Patterson, after the former champ slipped and fell to one knee.**

and he returned the same summer to administer a three-round beating to former British champion Brian London, who was hopelessly outclassed. With the draft call-up due at any time, Ali went to Germany a month later to fight their champion Karl Mildenberger, a southpaw who set him all sorts of problems until the twelfth round, when he crumbled.

That just about cleaned up the European scene for Ali and he returned to the States for a match with Cleveland Williams, who had troubled Liston a few years earlier. But Williams was no match for Ali, who displayed his most dazzling form since becoming champion to halt him in three rounds. Ali moved on to the unification showdown with Terrell at Houston's Astrodome where, cruelly, in front of some 37,000 fans, he tormented him for fully 15 rounds, asking repeatedly: 'What's my name, what's my name?' But the draft was closing in on Ali. A month later he met the veteran Zora Folley, a top contender for a decade, and retired him in seven painful rounds. It was to be his last fight for three-and-a-half years because three weeks later he refused to accept his induction. He was an outcast.

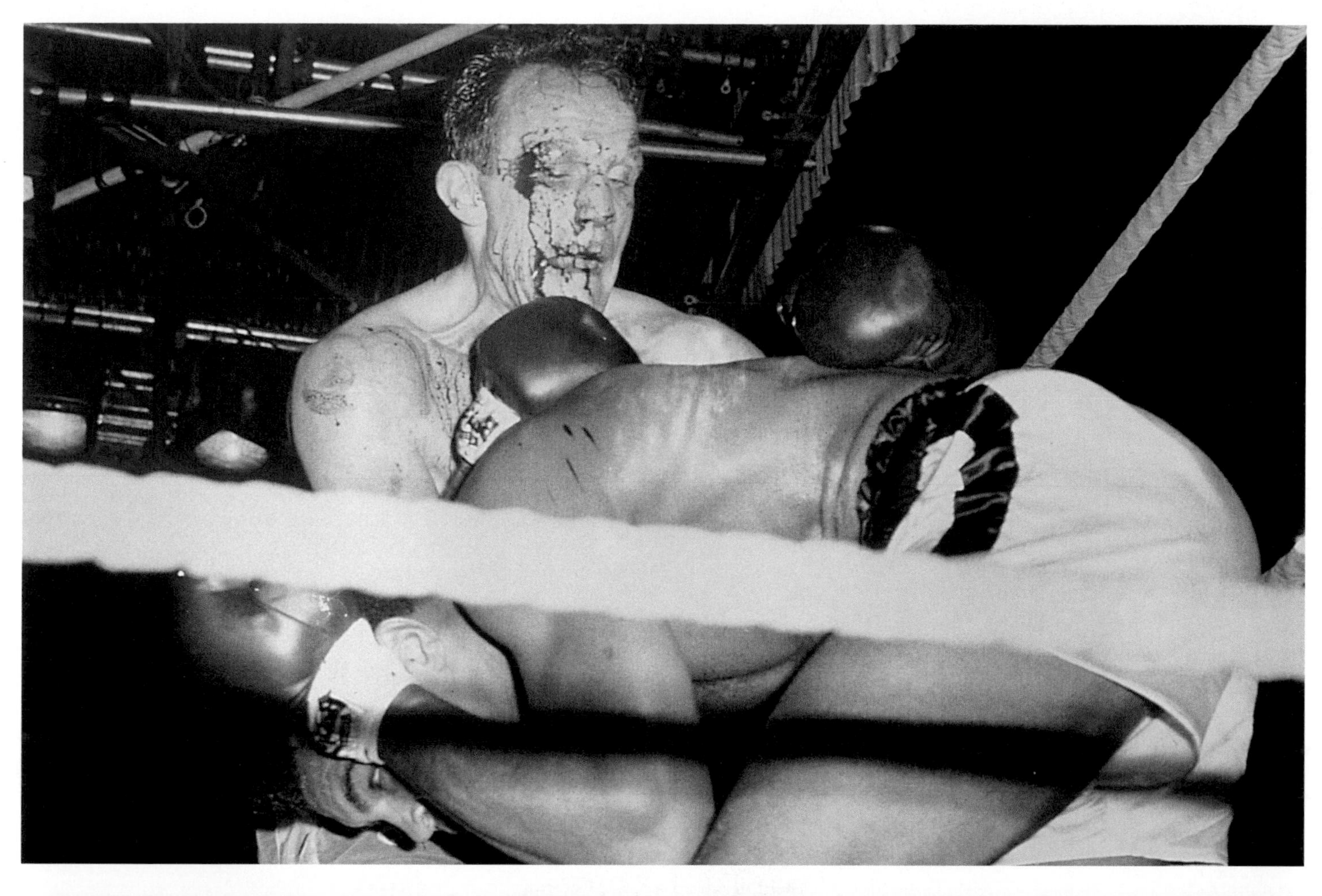

**Far Left: 25 November, 1965. World Heavyweight bout: Patterson vs. Ali.**

**Left: 21 May, 1966, London. World Heavyweight title: Henry Cooper vs. Muhammad Ali.**

**Below Left: 6 August, 1966. World Heavyweight bout: Brian London vs. Muhammad Ali.**

**Right: 10 September, 1966, Frankfurt, Germany. Muhammad Ali beats contender Karl Mildenberger for the world title.**

**Left: 14 November, 1966, Houston. While challenger Cleveland Williams lies sprawled on the canvas, Ali raises his arms in victory.**

**Right: 6 February, 1967. Ali punches challenger Ernie Terrell in the third round of their Heavyweight Championship fight at Houston's Astrodome.**

**Left: 22 March, 1967, New York. Ali stands over the fallen challenger Zora Folley in the 7th round of their title bout at Madison Square Garden.**

# the OUTCAST

'I SAID I WAS THE GREATEST NOT THE SMARTEST,' WAS ALI'S RESPONSE TO THE NEWS THAT HE had failed two draft tests. As an 18-year-old he had registered for the armed forces shortly before the 1960 Olympics but, as he later argued in his defense: 'I was a Christian then and knew nothing about Islam and had I been drafted then I would have gone.' When, predictably, Ali refused induction in April 1967, he was just 25 years old, at his absolute prime, and destined for his toughest fight — against the US Government.

He was fined $10,000 and given a five-year prison sentence, suspended on appeal. American whites called him a coward 'nigger scum' and directed even worse derogatory remarks toward him. Both the Army and his sponsoring group attempted to convince him he wouldn't actually be involved in warfare, that he would spend his time giving exhibitions for the troops and generally bolstering morale. But he wouldn't have anything to do with their pleas. 'We did it for Joe Louis,' an Army chief reassured him. 'Yea, and look where he is now,' replied Ali, mindful that the old champ had fallen on hard times. 'Clay Hated By Millions' read one headline, and some ex-champs went on record as saying he was a disgrace to the country and the sport.

To complete his humiliation, Ali was also stripped of his title and the World Boxing Association instigated a series of eliminators to determine a new champion. Ali insisted: 'Everyone knows who the real champ is regardless of who wins,' but business is business and the fact remained that he was in the wilderness. So, too, was Liston but for other reasons. He wasn't even invited to take part because months earlier he had

**Previous Page: Muhammad Ali addresses a Black Muslim Annual Convention.**

**Left: 27 April, 1967, Houston. Surrounded by newsmen and admirers, Ali looks skyward as he leaves Federal court in Houston, after a federal judge tossed out his last legal effort to avoid being drafted into the Army.**

**Below Left: 21 March, 1967, New York. The Madison Square Garden marquee shows the last advertising of a heavyweight championship fight at the Garden before the future bouts shift to the new Madison Square Garden later in 1967.**

**Right: 5 April, 1967, New York. Floyd Patterson and Muhammad Ali make a handsome picture as the two sluggers sign to meet for the World Heavyweight Championship that Ali holds and that Patterson once held.**

**Far Right: February 1968. Muhammed Ali gestures characteristically as he talks to a crowd of some 1,500 students at California State stadium. Ali remarked that violence in the streets would not aid the Negros' cause and remarked, 'Rioting in the ghettos is like a bull running into a locomotive.'**

been KO'd sensationally by Leotis Martin in nine rounds. Liston, who was alleged to have underworld connections, was later found shot dead in his apartment. Joe Frazier, best of the prospects not to have fought Ali so far, refused to participate. Instead, as the title was carved up, he won another version and later went on to claim the overall crown. Jimmy Ellis, former junior clubmate of Ali's in Louisville, beat white hope Jerry Quarry — later to figure prominently in Ali's comeback — to claim the WBA title, then defended against Patterson. Ellis was then stopped in four rounds by Frazier in a unification match.

Meanwhile, Ali's lawyers worked night and day without success to get his boxing licence reinstated,

**Right: 26 October, 1970, Atlanta. Mrs. Coretta King and Dr. Ralph Abernathy honor Muhammad Ali after his win over Jerry Quarry.**

as well as pressuring the government to rescind the sentence. Every knock-back, however, saw a new cloud of depression descend on the already dispirited ex-champ, who entertained serious thoughts of quitting the sport which had been his life. What lifted the cloud and rescued him to an extent was the new feeling of futility among American whites and blacks alike as the Vietnam war dragged on senselessly, cutting the country's lifeblood down in their prime. Suddenly, Ali was no longer an outcast, especially among the young people. In fact, he was a hero again and he began to earn a living of sorts on a nationwide tour of colleges. He also preached on the virtues of Islam.

Sadly, his new religious views clashed head-on with those of his wife and, as she grew weary of Ali's demands that she conform, the marriage crumbled after less than a year. Within months of exile, however, a new Mrs. Ali appeared. She was a pretty

**Left: 1 April, 1972, Tokyo, Japan. Muhammad Ali vs. Mac Foster. Ali won on points after 15 rounds.**

teenager called Belinda who had been born into the Muslim faith and practised her religion devoutly. She was an ideal soul-mate for Ali and she was to bear him four children, including twin daughters, in the next five years.

Though Ali's finances had dwindled to zero, boxing had also paid the price for his absence because there were no readymade crowd-pullers and this brought an end to the big pay-days promoters had enjoyed with him. For all the furore he had caused by his religious and military declarations promoters were working side by side with his lawyers to get him back in the ring. They reasoned, correctly, that a showdown against Frazier — two unbeaten champions — would he the biggest selling fight of all time. But for all their effort in several states as the Sixties drew to a conclusion, they were thwarted by the respective authorities at every turn.

Both Ali and Frazier knew how much they needed each other; Frazier because there was no mammoth pay-day in the offing otherwise, and Ali to re-establish himself as the world's greatest. He was hardly rolling in money, anyway, with an ex-wife to support as well as his costly day-to-day finances. Publicly, Ali derided Smokin' Joe and privately, Frazier hated him, hated his slick way with words and vowed to button his lip once and for all. A good many other fighters had attempted the same but Frazier was different. The ex-slaughterhouseman from Philadelphia was fired up as never before because of the taunts. Yet for all the vitriol that flowed, there was much mutual respect between Frazier and Ali, who once in desperation even offered his services to the champion as a hired sparring partner for a few hundred dollars. But both were unbeaten and both knew there would be far more than a fistful of dollars at stake if they ever met in the ring.

Three barren years went by for Ali before the breakthrough came, first in June 1970 when his prison sentence was reversed, then three months later in Atlanta, Georgia, whose Mayor, Sam Massell, granted him a boxing licence. The Mayor was persuaded by Senator Leroy Johnson, the first black man ever to be elected in the Deep South — that it would be a good thing for the city, even though the state of Georgia had previously rejected an application. Johnson even joined the promotional team responsible for drumming up publicity. Not that any was needed. There was only one small snag: Frazier. Smokin' Joe, who saw himself as something of a soul singer, had gone on tour with his band and was in no condition to face Ali, ring-rusty or not. There was a solution, though, in the shape of Jerry Quarry, the talented Irish-American white fighter who was also a top contender. In fact, a black versus white contest in Atlanta, a predominantly black city, served only to add spice to the momentous occasion.

But could Ali really turn the clock back and recapture the dazzling brilliance with which he had illuminated the heavyweight division as no other before him? He certainly looked the part in training and sparring. Any surplus weight had been stripped off and his speed of foot and hand was still there. But the answer, on an incredible night in Atlanta, was not that easy coming.

Quarry could bang, of that there was no doubt, and he was always active, but could he really spoil Ali's big day and stage one of the greatest upsets in heavyweight history?

Along with such black ringside celebrities as Diana Ross, Sidney Poitier and Bill Cosby, part if not the full answer came on 26 October, 1970, as Ali climbed through the ropes for his first taste of serious action in 42 months. A sell-out crowd of thousands greeted his arrival ecstatically, and with closed-circuit TV ready to monitor his every punch, Ali was well and truly back in the spotlight. Such was the din that Ali's name could not be heard as the fighters were introduced, and it was almost as overpowering as Ali waded into Quarry from the first bell, whipping out combinations and jabs just like the old days. But it certainly wasn't like the old days in round two as an already wearying Ali slowed the tempo. Quarry, one of the best counter-punchers around, started catching him as his confidence grew and he finished the round well on top.

Ali's lack of serious ringwork showed, yet he came out as if rejuvenated in round three and caught Quarry with a flurry of punches. Blood began pouring from a cut over his opponent's eye, which encouraged Ali to step up an already cracking pace. At the end of the round Quarry trudged back to his corner as if knowing his night's work had been cut short. It had.

**Left: January, 1971, New York. A photographic portrait of Muhammad Ali in action.**

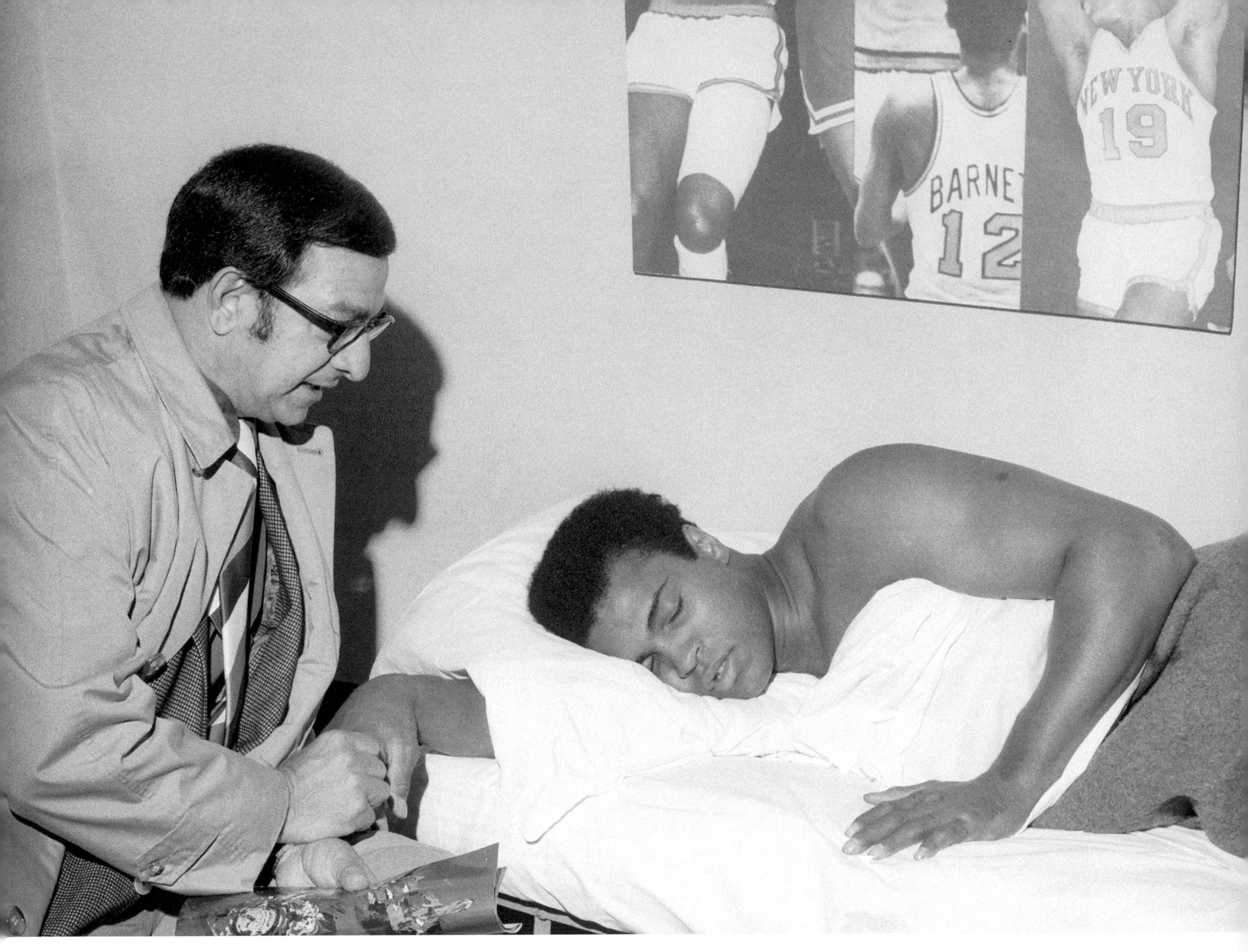


There were flaws, serious flaws in Ali's timing, and his legendary speed simply wasn't there for periods. 'I'm shocked that I was so tired,' admitted Ali, but had he really deteriorated that much or, was he simply shrugging off the lethargy which had overcome the greatest fighting machine ever assembled?

In fairness, Ali had been under immense pressure, and not just with his ring return. His wife Belinda had produced twin girls prematurely and there was no guarantee they would survive. She had already lost a son, who lived for only a few minutes, so there was additional cause for concern. Also, he and Bundini maintained they were shot at one morning in Atlanta while they were putting the finishing touches to his training. Ali also said he had received threatening phone calls warning him not to fight Quarry. For all

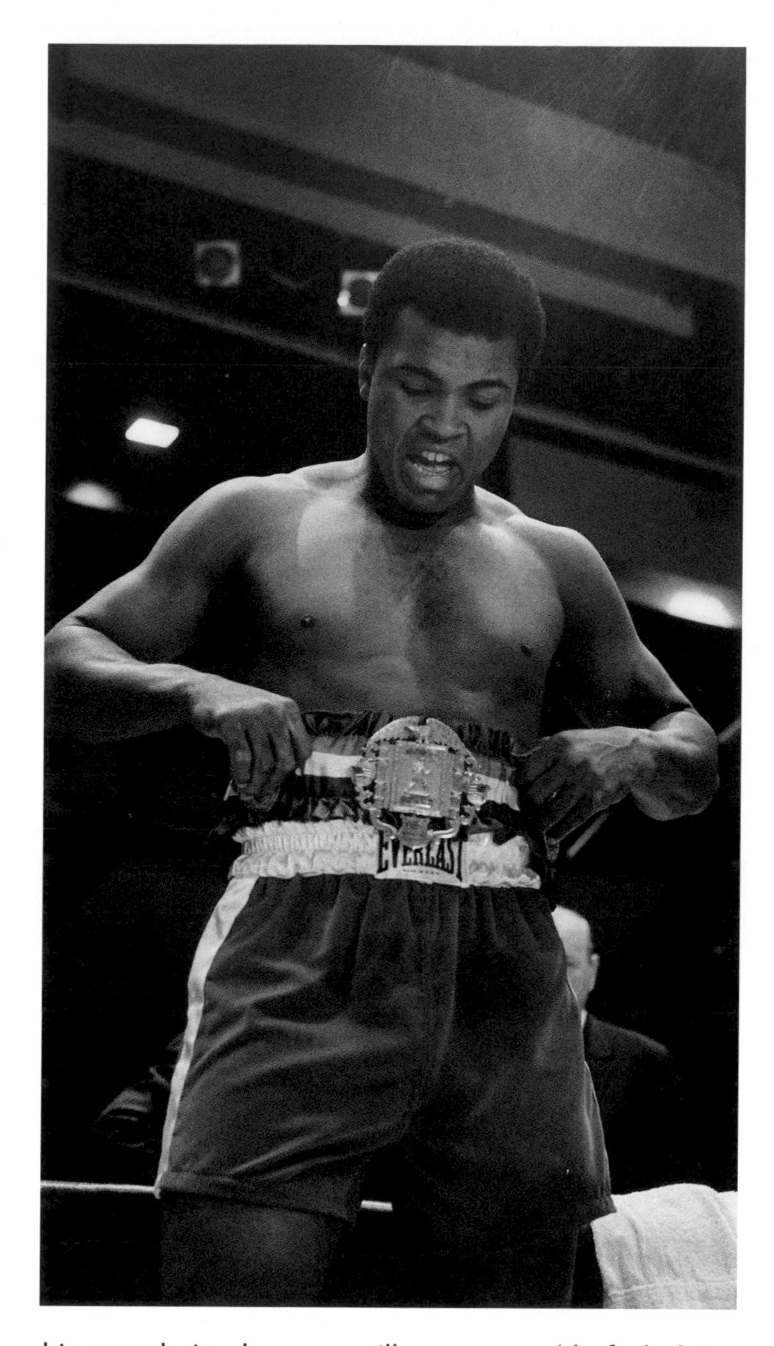


his popularity, he was still seen as a 'draft-dodging nigger' in some quarters. There were even death threats but, happily, they amounted to nothing and Belinda called before the fight to say she was back at their Philadelphia home with the twins. There was further good news when the state of New York also granted him a boxing licence. He was back in business but, for all that, Dundee and Ali still had to find out whether his deterioration was permanent before tackling Frazier.

They couldn't have chosen a tougher examination than Oscar Bonavena, the rough-and-tumble, chunk-of-muscle Argentinian with long Samson-like locks who fought with elbows, head and any other part of his anatomy that served as a weapon. He was as horrible as he looked and was married to a hooker. He would later die in a street brawl.

'If I can't beat him, I'm not ready for Joe,' said Ali, while the Frazier camp were convinced he was tossing away a fortune for both fighters. After all, Bonavena had decked Frazier twice in their first fight and gone the distance twice with the unbeaten champion, giving him the hardest scraps of his life. But Ali was adamant and for a near-$1 million purse, he took on Bonavena at New York's Madison Square Garden on 7 December the same year.

He nearly lived to regret it as the uncompromising Argentinian with the cast-iron jaw handled everything Ali threw at him and staged a late, dangerous rally that could have been conclusive. Unfortunately for him, Ali again dug deep into his resources in the fifteenth round and became the first man to KO Bonavena. Now for Frazier, but was Ali being premature? Surely he needed another warm-up fight or two to fine-tune his body? It was not to be. Exactly three months later, back at the Garden in front of another sell-out crowd, the two warriors settled their differences in a showdown billed as 'The Greatest Fight of the Century.'

Ali's last-round success over Bonavena and the manner in which he achieved it convinced him he could take Frazier at any time. After all, he'd beaten the time barrier and, anyway, he had the supreme conviction that he was invincible. But Frazier had the same unquenchable lust for greatness, he also yearned to be overall heavyweight supremo.

**Left: 4 March, 1971, New York. Strapping on his championship title belt at a pre-fight physical Ali declares, 'Joe Frazier doesn't have the real belt. How can you have two champions?'**

**Far Left: 8 March, 1971, New York. Manager Angelo Dundee sits by Muhammad Ali as he takes a nap a few hours after weigh-in at Madison Square Garden.**

**Right: 19 July 1972, Dublin, Ireland. Muhammad Ali celebrates his win over Al 'Blue' Lewis, an 11th round stoppage.**

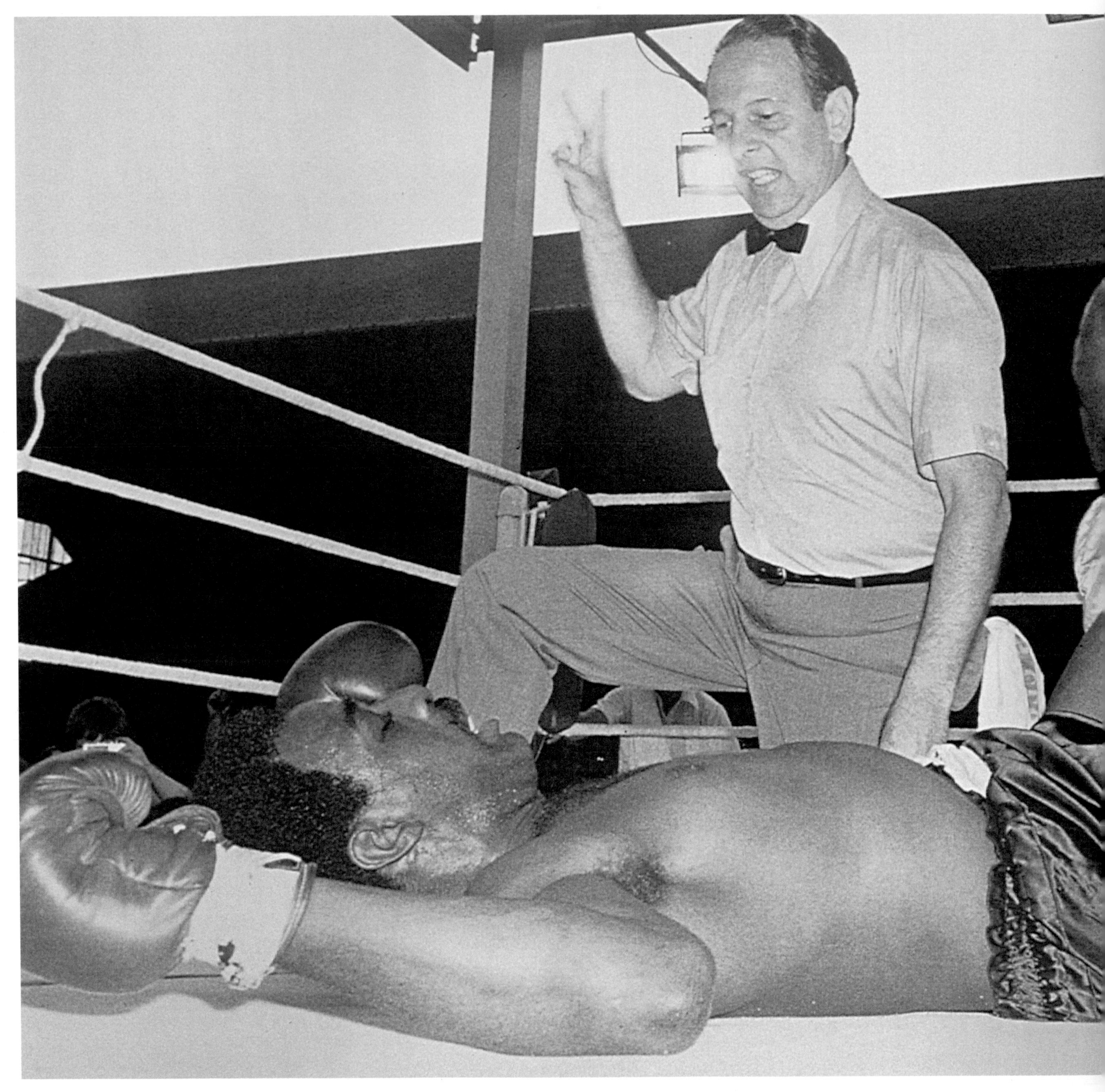

It really did have all the makings of a classic event — and the two undefeated champions obliged. Tickets for the Garden were sold out weeks in advance and a 25,000 crowd paid over $1,300,000, a record. Celebrities abounded throughout the arena, transforming the night into a glittering showbiz event. For the first time Ali topped the $1 million prize mark and Frazier, who had never been able to draw big money, was on the same $2,500,000 deal. But once they got to work the cash was far from their minds. Ali, with an eye to enhancing his own legendary status, knew he needed a great opponent, a Mount Everest to conquer, just as he did when he took the title from Liston. Joe Louis had his Schmeling, Robinson had his Basilio. . . and Ali had his Frazier.

But Frazier the gunslinger was oblivious to legends. He hated all that Ali stood for and his loathing, his burning desire to muzzle the Louisville Lip was ultimately his undoing. Smokin' Joe was born to fight. Reared in South Carolina, he packed his bags as a teenager in search of the big-time and headed for Philadelphia, home of the world's toughest fighters. Everything was geared around punishing nightly training sessions, and Frazier responded admirably, even at that early age. He took the first job he stumbled across — in a slaughterhouse — to cover his rent and gym fees, and legend has it that he actually killed some animals with his bare hands to stay in trim. By 1963 he was America's most feared amateur heavyweight and the following year in Tokyo he joined the Ali set by winning an Olympic gold. On his return he turned pro under the lovable, loyal Yancey 'Yank' Durham and soon punched his way into the top 10. His progress to the top, in the absence of Ali, was as inevitable as their clash at Madison Square Garden.

A full description of the fight would fill a book, such was its brutality and, perversely, its beauty. Frazier forced the fight from the off and early on it seemed

Right: 20 September, 1972, New York. Boxing Commissioner Edwin Dooley and challenger Floyd Patterson look on as Muhammad Ali, quoted as describing himself as 'trim, fast and ready to go,' weighs in preparatory to their scheduled 12-round heavyweight bout at Madison Square Garden.

ever, from Ali, who had promised to crawl across the ring if Frazier won. 'You the champ,' said Ali, as they embraced each other. 'We don't do no crawling,' replied Frazier. 'We both bad niggers — we don't do no crawling.'

The end for Ali? Or was it? Would he truly surrender or did he have it in him to surmount this new challenge, to regain his title? It was to take him three-and-a-half painful, frustrating years, the same length of his exile, to find the answer, to prove he truly was The Greatest, and his mettle was tested every step of the way, especially by Ken Norton. Ali returned to the ring four months after the worst night of his life to beat his old pal and sparring partner Jimmy Ellis with a twelfth-round stoppage. Then followed a succession of comeback fights, including a one-sided seventh-round stoppage against Quarry in which Ali virtually begged the referee to halt the slaughter. Then came an equally fatuous match against Patterson which was also concluded in the same round.

Britain's Joe Bugner, an Adonis-like, Hungarian-born heavyweight, was next, but though he traveled the full 12 rounds, he hardly pushed Ali all night. The next test, supposedly another warm-up, came in the form of Norton, but it was far from that. Norton, a top-tenner who had hardly set the scene alight, bemused Ali with his crossed-arms style and shattered him in the second round with a punishing right that broke his jaw. Ali was in agony and Dundee begged him to quit. But such was the great man's make-up that he insisted on soldiering on, only to lose a 12-round points decision. It was courage of the highest order but did Ali little good because he was confined to hospital to have the misshapen jaw wired up.

Now was the time to quit, surely, because, for the second time in two years, his invincibility had been shattered. But Ali was unmoved. He was convinced his

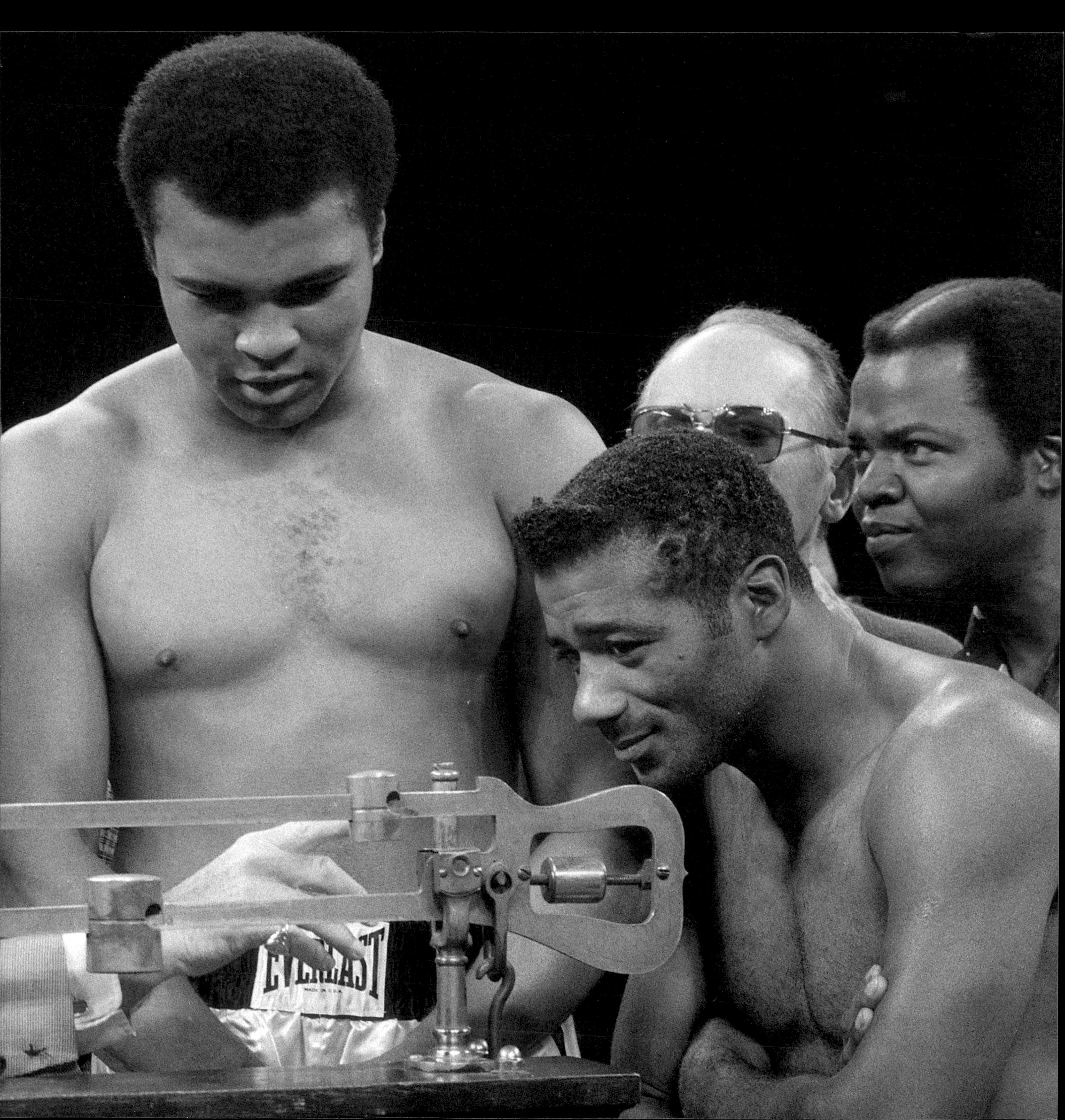

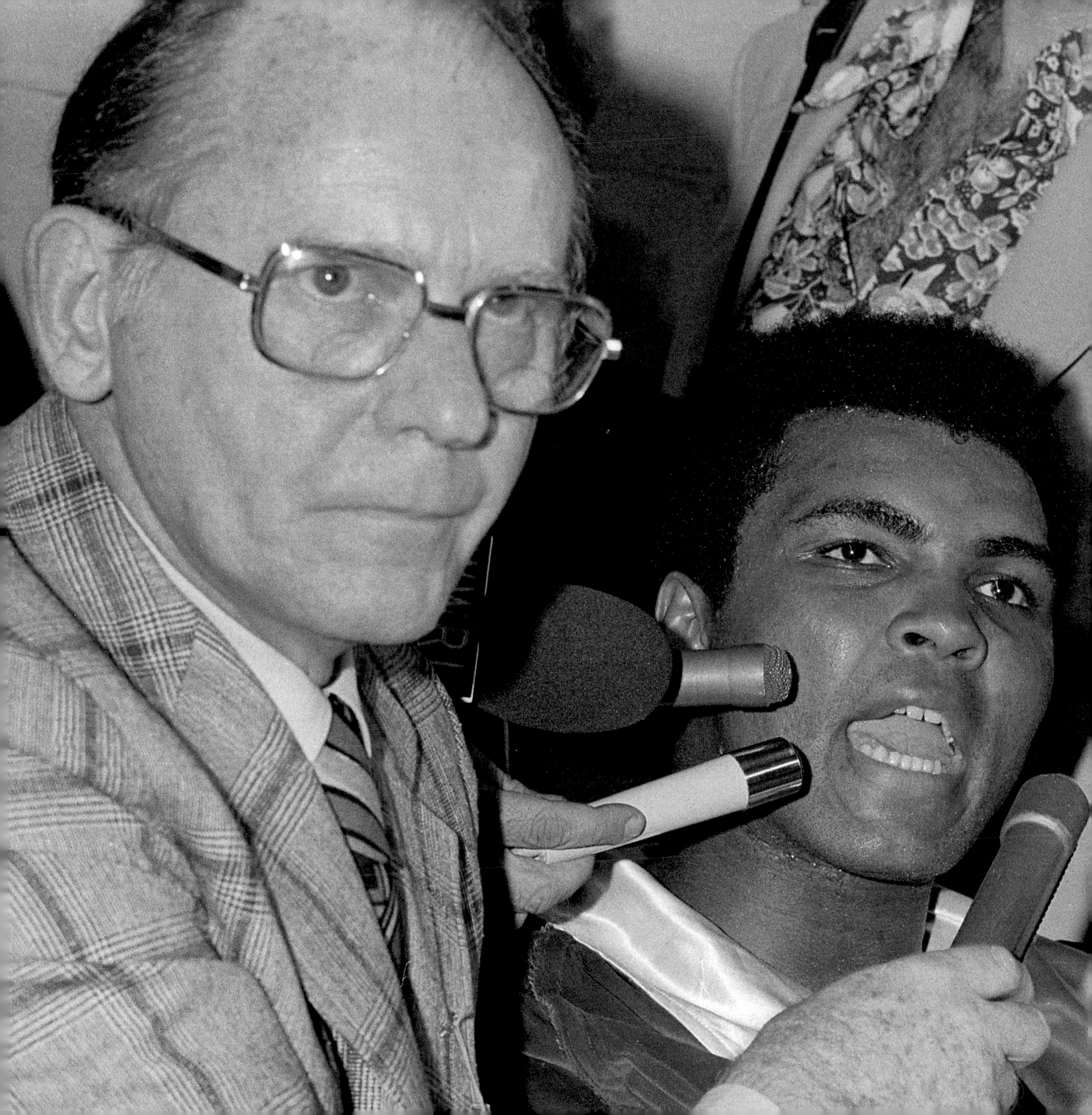

**Left: 10 May, 1973, Philadelphia. Muhammad Ali now thirty-one years old still aiming for the heavyweight title as he shows his left fist to the camera during an interview in Philadelphia.**

**Center Left: 27 June, 1973. Muhammad Ali vs Jerry Quarry. The fight was stopped by the referee after 7 rounds.**

**Far Left: 28 September, 1972. Muhammad Ali faces reporters after his fight with Floyd Patterson.**

destiny was to be The Greatest so, painstakingly, he began rebuilding his career yet again. His first exam, much against Dundee's wishes, was with the dangerous Norton. By this time George Foreman had hammered Frazier in two rounds to take the world title and his handlers knew there was only one pot of gold to look forward to — a showdown with Ali.

Ali had other things on his mind first, like revenge over Norton, and he stressed that Foreman and everyone else would have to wait. His chance came five months later, after his wired-up jaw, and his heart, had mended and, although he had to make do with a points win, at least he had avenged a sorry defeat. Ali went looking for more revenge three months later when he tackled Frazier and, with his old speed of foot back in evidence, beat him comfortably in a 12-round eliminator in New York. 'I've evened up two old scores and wiped out the bad taste of defeat,' said Ali. 'Now I'm thinking about retirement, about a life with my family and children.' But the decline was finally over and there was one more goal: the world championship. Ali was aiming for the stars yet again.

the

# SECOND COMING

## JUST THREE MONTHS OFF HIS THIRTY–THIRD BIRTHDAY AND ALI WAS READY TO WAGE WAR

on Foreman, the Colossus who looked even more formidable than the Liston of old. Conversely, just as Cassius Clay was deemed too young to match Liston, so boxing's afficionados felt Ali had regressed too far and was too old to stand up to the new monster. But the old Louisville Lip was convinced that his superior all-round ability could negate Foreman's thunderous power-punching, which lifted poor Frazier clean off the canvas when he took the title from him.

**Previous Page: Muhammad Ali in training for his fight against Al 'Blue' Lewis, Dublin, 1972.**

**Right: 30 October, 1974, Kinshasa, Zaire. Heavyweight Champ George Foreman, throws a left to the eye of Muhammed Ali during their title bout. This shot twisted Ali's face but not his direction.**

Such was the worldwide impact of the fight that Ali's manager Herbert Muhammad, via astute American promoter Don King, was able to negotiate with Zaire, an emerging African nation formerly called the Belgium Congo, to stage the richest promotion in history with $12 million being promised to cover costs and both fighters guaranteed nearly 50 percent. It was the first time a government had ever sponsored a title fight and, thanks to King and Herbert, it certainly wouldn't be the last.

Both fighters planned to wind up their training in Kinshasa, where the fight was being staged, a fortnight before the event, and Ali pulled what he felt was a master stroke by employing among his sparring partners Bossman Jones, a light-heavyweight who had worked with Foreman for several weeks. What he told Ali when questioned extensively about the world champion, however, should have persuaded him not to tackle Foreman. In Ali's intriguing autobiography *The Greatest*, Bossman tells him chillingly: 'The people accept George as a brute and they come to see him knock somebody out. George got the guns to do it. I see fighters who could stun you, who could knock you out, but George is the first one I been in the ring with I know can kill you. He may never kill nobody and I hope he never does, but he's got the power to kill, and he knows it. He has a special punch called the "anywhere" punch because anywhere it hits you, it breaks something inside you — a muscle, a bone, a shoulder, a finger, a rib.'

Bossman painted a formidable picture of the champion and when Ali asked about his weaknesses, Jones replied, 'He ain't got none.' When Ali asked if Bossman ever tagged him in training, Jones said: 'The sparring partners know better than to hit him. Once you hit him he'll tear your head off.' He also warned Ali that he couldn't get away with fighting on the ropes, as he had done in recent years: 'George knows how to

**Next Page: 30 October, 1974, Kinshasa, Zaire. George Foreman looks up from flat on his back after Muhammad Ali knocks him down in the 8th round.**

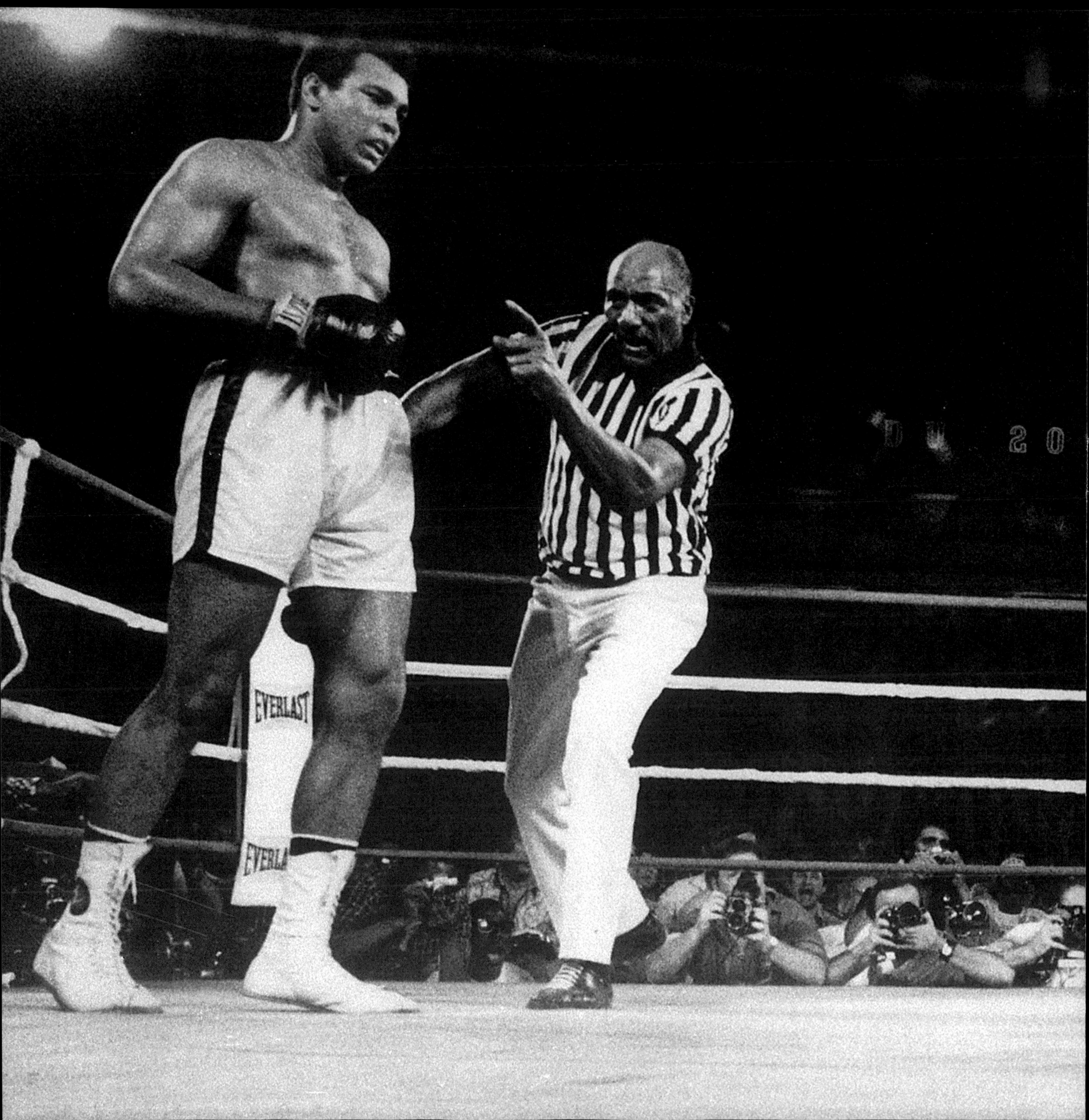
EVERLAST

M A I
EVERLAST
EVERLAST

corner a man and he can lift you up off your feet with one punch. If you lay on the ropes and rest, he's gonna break your ribs. He'll hit you on your way down or on your way up. By the time the referee gets there you might be beat to death. His most killing punch is a kidney punch. That's the only part of the body you can't tighten up.' As if to compound the enormous task facing Ali, Bossman added: 'George wants to win this fight bad. He wants to be accepted by the world as the real heavyweight champion. It's killing him. It's eating him up to have the title and have them still call Muhammed Ali, the People's Champion.'

For all that, Ali remained cocksure that his superior strategy would suffice. . . but then came a bombshell. With days to go before their showdown, Foreman sustained a nasty freak cut above his right eye, caught accidentally by an elbow while sparring. Ali's heart sank because he knew this would be his only chance to tackle Foreman. Fortunately Dick Sadler, Foreman's trainer, was an expert 'cuts' man and managed to seal the wound without the need for stitches. Two weeks later he was back in the ring sparring, his eye completely healed, and at 3.45am (9pm in New York) on his 55th day in Zaire, Ali stepped out to the greatest reception of his life. As he made his way to the ring for his date with destiny, the huge moonlit crowd began chanting 'Ali, Ali Bom a ye, Ali, Ali, Bom a ye'(it came out as 'boom ah yea' and meant 'Knock him down, kill him dead'). Ali danced around the ring, getting the feel of it and waving to the excited crowd. They loved him, loved his showmanship, and while Foreman failed to appear for fully 10 minutes, Ali used the time wisely, keeping warm and whipping up a crescendo of support.

When Foreman did arrive he stood, arms raised in the center of the ring, his massive frame silhouetted against the sky. He looked what he was: an absolute monster.

**Left: Foreman and Ali exchange blows during their bout for the World Heavyweight Championship.**

EVERLAST
ERLAST
LAST

Yet when the referee Zack Clayton called them together to administer the usual instructions, there was little to choose between their physiques. Ali was in magnificent shape for the greatest challenge of his life. He needed to be because right from the start he discovered Foreman was a lot smarter than he had given him credit for. When he started dancing to put space between them, Foreman cut the ring off with mammoth strides. He had been brilliantly schooled by old Archie Moore and Ali realized within a minute that his original stick-and-run plan just wouldn't work. 'I was having to take six steps to his two; and I realized I would be worn out long before him,' said Ali afterwards. Immediately he revised the plan and went against everything Bossman had warned him of by staying on the ropes. True, it was painful, almost pitiful to watch, as Foreman thundered in blows from all angles, especially into his body. Ali covered as best he could and indeed negated many of them with his arms, but it was inevitable some would get through, and they did toward the latter stages of the opening round.

Dundee pleaded with Ali to stay off the ropes during the interval, but he didn't know what Ali knew. 'I felt George's power and I knew why he had destroyed Frazier and Norton,' he said. Again in *The Greatest* Ali recalls vividly: 'My cornermen are screaming and I hear friends at ringside pleading for me to move out off the ropes, I taunt George, I goad him. "You ain't got no punch, you phony. Show me something, sucker," George roars in like a mob. He's throwing punches with tonnage I never thought a fist could carry. A crowbar in George's right hand crashes through my guard into my head, knocks me into the room of half-dream. My head vibrates like a tuning fork. Neon lights flash on and off. I've been here before. . . George's blows explode into my kidneys, my ribs, my head. I lean back, I slip and slide. I catch some on my arms, off

**Far Left: 1973. Muhammad Ali throws a punch at Ken Norton during one of their two bouts in this year.**

**Left: 25 January, 1974, New York. Muhammad Ali vs. Joe Frazier. Ali won after 12 rounds.**

my elbows, but I stay on the ropes. . . then near the end of the round I rise up and shoot quick, straight jabs and right crosses directly into George's head. POW! POW! POW! And I keep talking. I must not let him think his blows can stop me talking. "Sucker, is that all you got. Is that the hardest you can hit?"'

Ali was aware Foreman had forecast he would wipe him out in the third round the first time he'd had to travel that far in years — but he hung on through the biggest pounding he was ever to experience.

**Right: Ali holds a 'Wanted' poster of himself at his training camp.**

heart of a lion, a Joe Louis, a Rocky Marciano, the heart of a Joe Frazier?'

The answer was swift in coming. Foreman pawed out a left and, with lightning reactions, Ali responded with a right over the top, then a mighty straight right to the jaw. Almost in slow-motion, King Kong's eyes became glazed and just as slowly he crumpled to the canvas. At eight he rose and was back on his feet even as the ref reached 10. But it was too late. The greatest fighter in history had just won the 'Rumble in the jungle.' 'Ali proved his greatness time and again, not least in Kinshasa,' says Harry Mullan, Editor of Britain's weekly magazine *Boxing News*. 'He was six different fighters in one because he had the unique ability to adapt to every situation, to whatever obstacle was put in his way.'

Ali should have retired then and there, surrounded by thousands of adoring fans, but he just couldn't. He

**Left: 24 May, 1976, Munich. Ali vs. Richard Dunn. Ali prevailed in the 5th round with a knockout.**

loved being champion again, loved being called 'Champ.' Three defenses in as many months followed, the first against no-hoper Chuck Wepner just five months after his finest hour. Wepner should have been a pushover and Ali treated him as such, and got a tremendous shock when his 'rope-a-dope' bum of the month actually floored him. It was deemed a push but Wepner, bleeding profusely from cut eyes and mouth, kept coming back for more. Finally, he succumbed in the fifteenth round of a real battering. At the ringside in Cleveland that night was a young actor named Sylvester Stallone, a committed boxing fan who was full of admiration for Wepner's bravery. It gave him an idea, and the character 'Rocky' was born. The rest, as they say, is history.

Ali defended against Ron Lyle, a tough ex-convict, then Britain's Joe Bugner, before the inevitable third and final show-down with Frazier. If Ali had gone to

the gates of Hell and back in dismantling Foreman, then he surely entered Hades in the rubber match with his arch-enemy. He labeled it the 'Thrilla in Manila,' another great deal worked out with a nation's government for megabucks, and Ali freely admitted that he wanted to quit the fight at the end of the tenth round, such was the pain in his belly from Frazier's relentless onslaught. But the champ had never before quit in his life, so the hurting went on and on.

**Left: World Heavyweight Champion Muhammad Ali and his brother meet with President Ford at the White House. Ali said he liked the White House, and just might go after the job. Ford said there were times he'd be happy to let him have it.**

**Below Left: Ali shows off the $15,000 diamond-studded belt he was awarded as 'professional athlete of the year.'**

Far Right: 24 March, 1975, Richfield. Ali stands over his opponent, Chuck Wepner, after knocking him down against the ropes in the 15th round of their championship fight in Richfield.

Right: 17 June, 1975, Kuala Lumpur, Malaysia. Ali takes a break from a workout in the National Stadium to address spectators. He told the crowd that he had a new defensive tactic which he would use against British challenger Joe Bugner. The champ also said he was 99 percent sure he'd retire from the ring following the bout.

Something had to give because both men were giving and taking far too much punishment and in the end it was left to the fatherly figure of Eddie Futch, Frazier's veteran handler, to wave the white flag of surrender. 'You love a fighter like your own child,' Futch was prone to say, and somehow you always felt he meant it. He certainly did on an unbearably hot night in the Philippines. With just three minutes to go and with the by now non-Smokin' Joe arguing furiously in his corner, Futch called over referee Carlos Padilla and restored some sanity to the proceedings.

Frazier, his eyes mere slits gaping through huge swellings, cried the tears of a loser. Ali, too exhausted even to raise his arms in triumph, slumped to the floor and was tended to by the same men who would later throw him to the young lion called Larry Holmes, the same Larry Holmes who as a 21-year-old had helped

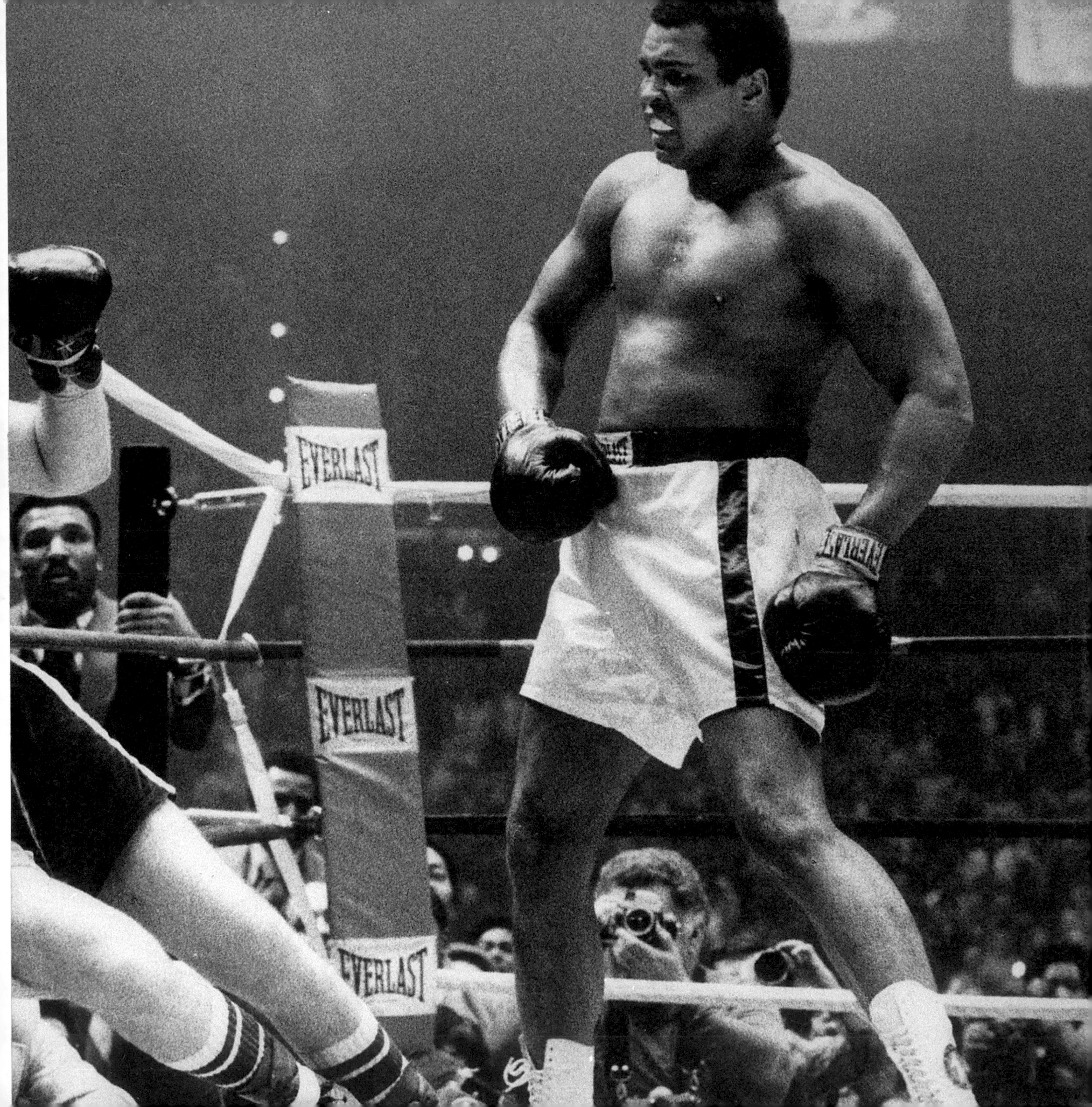
EVERLAST
EVERLAST
EVERLAST

# the DAY THE MUSIC DIED

## THE LAST THING ALI NEEDED WAS ANOTHER WAR, YET HE GOT ONE AGAINST BOGEY–MAN KEN NORTON.

The ex-marine was No.1 contender and his awkward style really troubled Ali. The venue for the match was the famous old Yankee Stadium and Norton had been fine-tuned by the wily Futch. After 15 torrid rounds, most observers were convinced they were seeing a new champion because Norton had boxed with aggression and guile. But Ali's immense reputation, plus his flashy finish to rounds, were enough to sway the decision his way. Just!

SANYO

Left: 26 July, 1976, Tokyo, Japan. Ali shouts 'Come on Inoki,' as the Japanese wrestler remains on the floor during the second round of their 15-round fight.

seemed he had faded from the scene when his crown was vacated. But the lure of the dollar and the limelight proved too much and one fateful morning in 1980, Ali set off once more for the gymnasium to prepare for a comeback fight against a peak Larry Holmes.

By this time his second marriage had also failed and, after leaving Belinda with their four children, including Muhammad Ali Jnr., in 1975, he was wed to a beautiful model, Veronique Porche, who caused a scandal when she appeared in Manila for Ali's third Frazier fight three years earlier. At the age of 38 he should have been playing with those kids and enjoying the trappings of wealth instead of reaching for an elusive dream by punishing himself and his body still further. Yet many believed him when he said he could return to topple his old sparring partner, by now installed as World Champion.

As ever, he talked a magnificent fight and he certainly looked the part when he clambered into the ring with not an ounce of fat showing after months of training. This was the legend who had led Liston a merry dance, had withstood Foreman's mighty salvos and even forced Frazier to surrender. But it was all an illusion and a weight-drained Ali was a mere shell with nothing left inside. Many fights since boxing began have left a nasty taste in the mouth and this was one, a contest no true fan likes to remember. If the music died the day Buddy Holly crashed out of the sky, as Don Maclean proclaimed in song, then this was the night boxing wept genuine tears after Ali's 10-round humiliation.

Ali clowned right up to the first bell, but could do nothing as Holmes took him apart systematically. Even he must have been horrified at Ali's ineptitude, his total inability to muster up a combination, to defend, to even shuffle. Shamble more like. By the seventh Holmes, as ruthless as his nickname the 'Easton

**Above: 27 August, 1976, Washington D.C. Secretary of State Henry Kissiger and Muhammad Ali appear to be engaged in some serious negotiating at a reception. Both men attended the World Boxing Association awards dinner.**

boxed on for three years. If God had wanted me to quit earlier I would have. There's a reason for everything and I have no regrets. You have to weigh good with bad and I've had a full life, experienced the lot. I have more peace of mind now than ever. Wish I could talk better, but the brain is alert. I've got more attuned to the things around me in the last few years. You know, like deaf people can maybe feel the ground rumbling, I'm like that.'

Would he have beaten, say, Mike Tyson, in his prime? Just watch the video of Cassius Clay whipping Liston, of Ali toppling Foreman. Watch his fight almost to the death against Frazier. He'd have beaten anyone. Time and again Muhammad Ali proved he was The Greatest, the smartest. But it still wasn't enough for the warrior who transformed heavyweight boxing. He transcended the thud and blunder and gave us sheer poetry. If only he'd remembered his lines a little better.

Ali's marriage to Veronique Porche had yielded two daughters, Hana (1976) and Laila (1979), giving him the impressive total of eight children — seven girls and a boy. His relationship with fourth wife Yolanda, more commonly known as Lonnie and a graduate of Vanderbilt University who started cooking for him when he was sick, survived the revelation that he'd

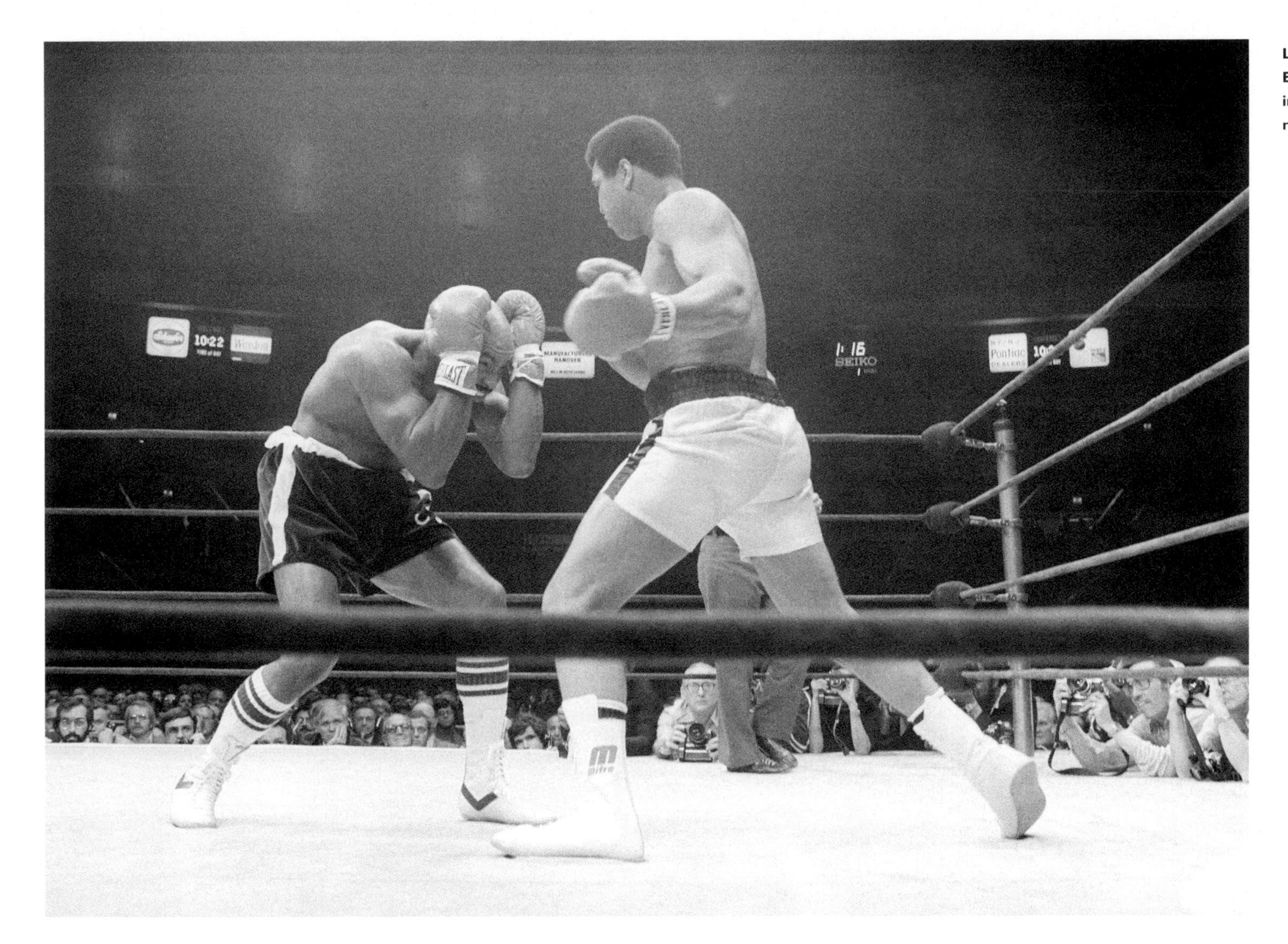


**Left: 29 September 1977. Earnie Shavers covers up during the first round of his match with Muhammad Ali.**

strayed, and was cemented in 1991 when the couple adopted a son, Asaad. The contented trio retired to a life of relative seclusion on his farm in Berrien Springs, Michigan, where Ali — his mental faculties seemingly unimpaired — slowly came to terms with his physical problems.

But seclusion is almost impossible when you're one of the world's most recognizable figures. This became clear one afternoon in December 1991 when, while heading home in his Rolls-Royce, he passed a car with its bonnet raised; a group of college students gathered helplessly, their journey interrupted. Ali's arrival at the side of the road caused something of a stir, the students (who'd not even been born as he hit his boxing heyday) standing in total awe as he untangled a set of jump leads he'd found in his car boot. He attempted to restart the stalled vehicle as passing vehicles honked their salute. One car even swerved out of the fast lane to stop, reverse and deliver a greeting: 'Ali, we love you! You are the greatest!' The three-time world heavyweight champion responded by blowing kisses.

Thankfully, the possibility of an accident was averted since, having failed in his attempt to get the stricken car started, he departed the scene with two students on board, having vowed to get them back to

**Right: 15 February, 1978, Las Vegas. Muhammad Ali vs. Leon Spinks. Spinks beat Ali on points after 15 rounds.**

campus. When one asked for an autograph, Ali simply signed a pamphlet on Islam and offered his cheek for a chaste kiss; on receiving it, he fell back as if poleaxed by a straight left before smiling a farewell.

One of Ali's past opponents made news again in October 1994. Jerry Quarry had faced Muhammad in the ring on two occasions, the first when he'd been the unfortunate man in the Atlanta ring in October 1970 when the former world title holder stormed back after being stripped of his crown. Despite lasting just three rounds on that occasion, Quarry faced Ali again in June 1972 when the fight was once more stopped, this time in the seventh. Though Ali had emerged the victor on both occasions, it was the vanquished Quarry who showed compassion by forming a foundation to research the link between boxing and brain damage. Quarry's mission statement mentioned that three members of his family who had turned to professional boxing had suffered permanent disablement, but his former opponent was also clearly in his thoughts.

The pair had more in common than many realized. Quarry had exhibited signs of dementia as early as 1982, and a neuropsychologist who'd examined him later in the decade estimated that boxing had aged him by some 30 years. The name for his disorder was dementia pugilistica, the effects of which were exhibited through symptoms of the better-known

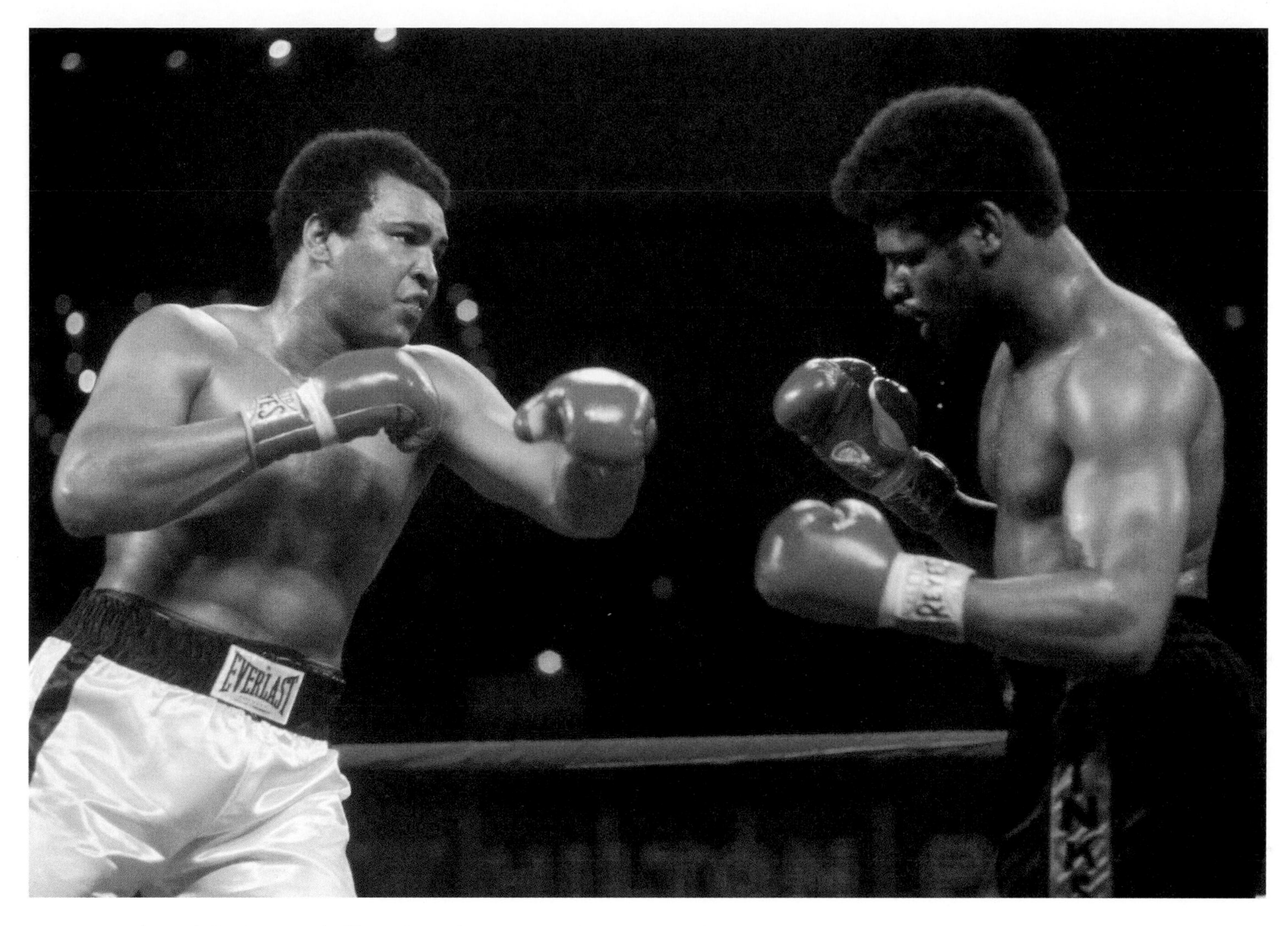


**Left: Muhammad Ali and Leon Spinks during ring action at the Las Vegas Hilton Pavilion.**

Parkinson's and Alzheimer's. Together, they cause both loss of memory and motor movement.

He spotlighted the lack of extensive research on this subject, plus the lack of a pension plan for permanently injured boxers — a crucial point, given that Quarry was surviving on benefits. Having fought on past the age it was safe to do so but unable to afford retirement, he'd pocketed just $1,050 for his final fight in 1992 in Colorado, a state where no boxing licence was required, compared with a $338,000 payday when facing Ali for the first time. 'My goals are to start a research program to learn more about how to treat and care for the injured athletes,' said Quarry. 'This would include a building or buying a facility for care and therapy. The government and the medical profession also need to be educated on how to safeguard all sports to prevent brain damage. Maybe some day we will develop regular screening for all athletes who apply for an amateur or professional license to compete in contact sports.'

The foundation announced its intentions via news releases in sports magazines and newspapers worldwide, starting off by sponsoring charity events. It would not now be long, however, before Quarry's better-known and more successful opponent re-emerged in his own right.

If Muhammad Ali had been absent from the headlines for the best part of a decade since his illness was

**Right:** Muhammad Ali has a solemn look as he sits in his corner and hears that he lost his heavyweight title to Leon Spinks by a split decision.

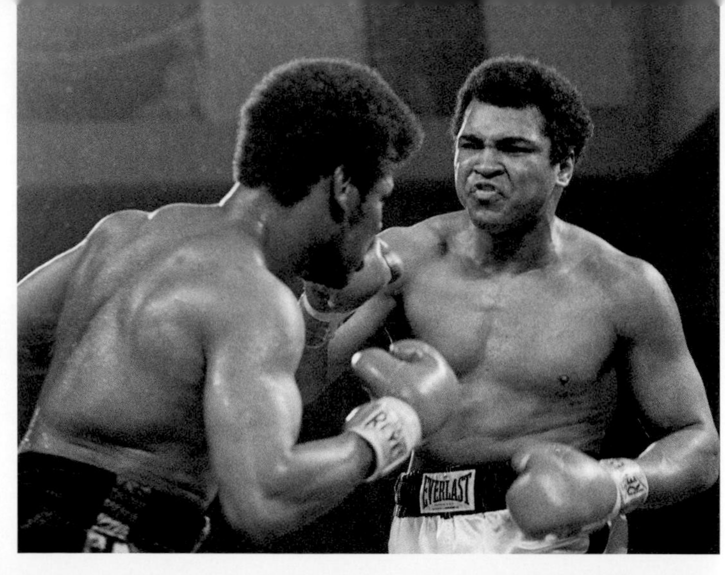


**Far Right:** Ali starts right to the head of challenger Leon Spinks in the 7th round.

**Right:** United Nations Secretary-General Kurt Waldheim accepts one of two 'paintings for peace' from and executed by Muhammad Ali. The works of art, to be on permanent display at the UN, were presented in honor of the Year of the Child.

**Left: Muhammad Ali relaxes at home with his daughter, September 1980.**

diagnosed, then 1996 would go down as the year that put him right back on the media map. It was suitable, too, that this was to happen at the Olympic Games, the event where, back in 1960 in Rome, he'd stolen the limelight as young light-heavyweight Cassius Clay.

His triumph then had been tempered with sorrow. Legend had it he'd thrown the hard-won medal into the Ohio river after being refused service at a diner, declaring 'I was the champion of the Olympics, the man with the gold medal... and it didn't mean nuthin'.' Nevertheless, the following years had seen him build a legend on that first successful step on the world stage. The pain of rejection had encouraged him to fight for his beliefs as hard as he fought for sporting honours, rejecting his slave name and challenging the prejudice inherent in American society. And it was for this as much as his ring record that he was remembered.

The athletes from 197 countries who gathered in Atlanta's Olympic Stadium had earlier recalled another son of the South, civil rights campaigner Dr. Martin Luther King. His widow Coretta was in attendance

**Right: Larry Holmes and Muhammad Ali trade blows during their heavyweight championship bout at Caesars Palace.**

**Far Right: 2 February, 1981, New York. Jack Dempsey takes a poke at Muhammad Ali during the first Thurman Award Dinner of the Association for the Help of Retarded Children. The award was presented to Dempsey, Ali, Billy Martin, Senator Bill Bradley, Ralph Kiner, Cliff Robertson, Ethel Kennedy and Munson's widow, Diana.**

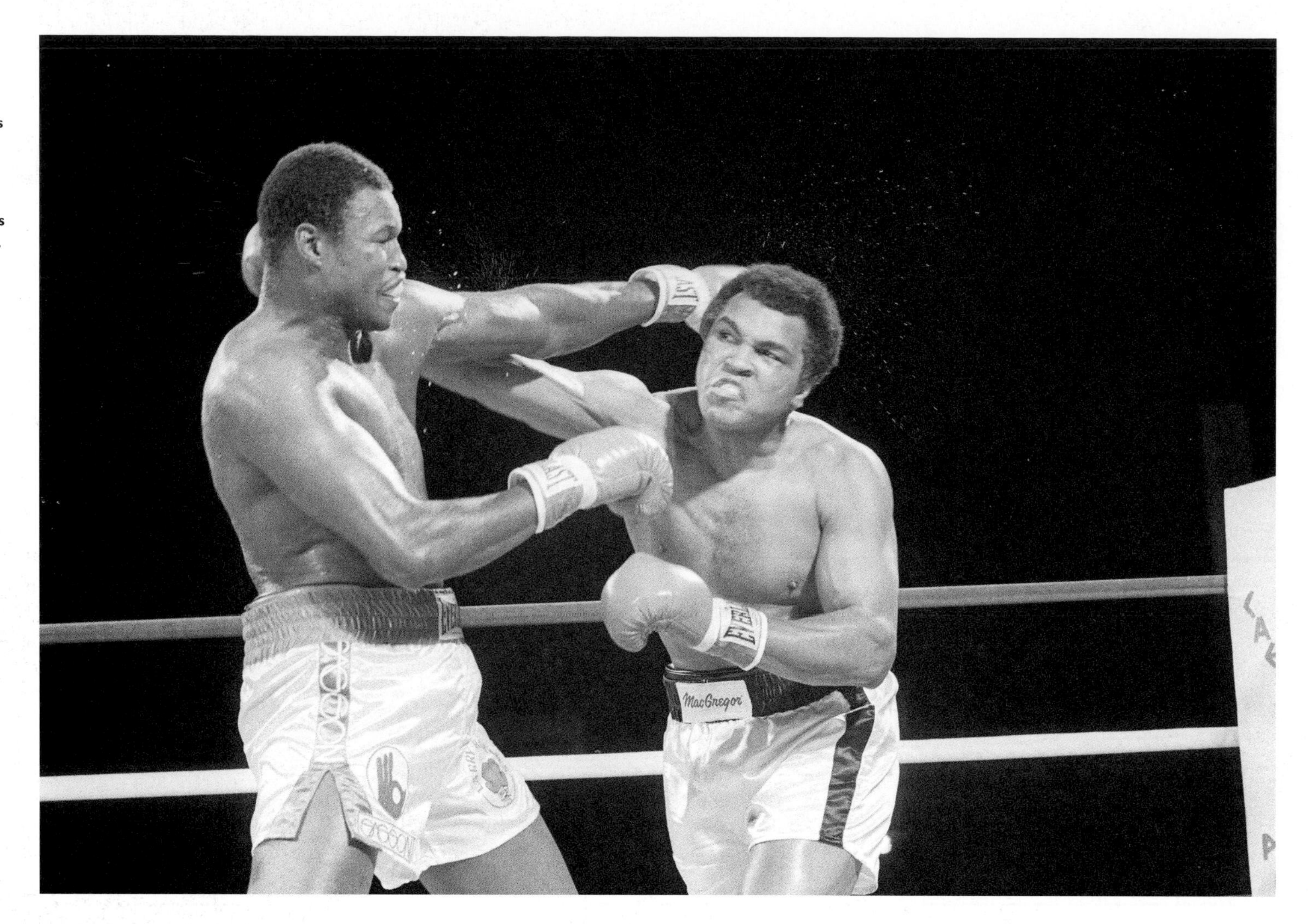


documentary film *When We Were Kings*. This could justly claim to have been longer in the making than almost any other celluloid documentary — but the results, by common consent, were spectacular. Director Leon Gast had filmed Ali and Foreman's title fight in Zaire back in 1974, but had lacked the funds to complete it. In point of fact, he'd intended to cover a three-day pop concert that preceded the fight, but this flopped when the match was delayed six weeks due to Foreman sustaining a cut when sparring.

Gast must have been glad he stuck around. To add to the sense of perspective, he intercut contributions by the likes of Spike Lee, biographer Thomas Hauser and other contemporary 1990s figures to leaven the ringside commentary by Norman Miler and George Plimpton. Don King was in evidence, having extorted a $10 million purse from Zaire's President Mobutu.

But the real star was Ali, who had started playing mind games with favorite Foreman long before they reached the ring. An early press conference saw Ali come out with the classic line 'I'm so mean I make medicine sick.' And with time on his hands due to Foreman's injury, he continued to weight the psychological scales until they were very much in his favor. Ali clearly won the crown outside the ring as much as the 27 minutes he spent in it.

The film's producer David Sonenberg paid him a warm tribute. Muhammad Ali, he said, was 'more than

SECURITY
OFFICER

**Right: Muhammad Ali, 1985. His legend and glory have not faded with retirement from thr ring.**

**Left: New York, 1986. Muhammad Ali and Joe DiMaggio stand side by side after receiving Liberty Medals at Ellis Island.**

Someone who also fancied playing the young Ali was actor-pop singer Will Smith. The *Independence Day* star was reported to be lined up as lead in a $30 million Warner Bros epic, with Jon (*Batman*) Peters producing. The project had been in development for nearly ten years, with Oliver Stone lined up at one point to direct, and if true the skinny Smith would have to put on an estimated 40 pounds for the role.

It was perhaps surprising that Smith hadn't been lined up in a singing capacity to appear at an October benefit concert in Los Angeles for the Muhammad Ali World Healing Project — but he wasn't missed from a bill boasting the likes of Prince and Celine Dion. 'I wish people would love everybody else the way they loved me,' commented Ali, who went on to explain his aim of raising money for existing charities working to combat prejudice and bigotry.

**Right: 1984. Friends Muhammad Ali and Sylvester Stallone play boxing.**

Though Muhammad Ali had opened his professional career in his home town of Louisville in 1960, his last fight there had been in November 1961, when he'd knocked out Willi Bosmanoff in the seventh round. Just short of 36 years later, he returned to the ring in Louisville for three one-minute rounds of 'mock boxing' for a charitable donation of $50,000.

The pageant in September 1997 was to celebrate the first year of the Ali Cup, an international amateur competition which attracted 96 competitors from fully 30 countries. 'We hope this great event will put Louisville on the map as a center for boxing,' commented mayor Jerry Abramson. Indeed, the Cup won instant official backing when it was announced its results would determine the members of the US boxing team at the following month's World Championship in Hungary. Another welcome spin-off was the raising of some $1 million to go towards a museum and education center in Louisville to bear Ali's name.

The Ali Cup festivities were also notable for the presence of several other former heavyweight champions, notably Jimmy Ellis, Ken Norton, Evander Holyfield and Mike Tyson. The latter pair were no strangers, having met a mere matter of months earlier when Tyson had left the ring in disgrace after

**Left: Two great boxers with The Greatest — Joe Frazier, George Foreman and Muhammad Ali.**

biting off a chunk of his opponent's ear. They had responded to Ali's invitation in the hope that the incident — which cost Tyson £3 million and his boxing licence, revoked for a year — could be put formally in the past. Holyfield's statement read: 'The meeting is a great way to cleanse the sport of boxing of an incident we all regret.'

Ali's sporting exploits — not to mention his courage in returning to the public gaze — were recognized in 1997 by the Arthur Ashe Award for Courage. He was the fifth person to receive the accolade named after the late, great Afro-American tennis player, to whom Ali paid the following tribute: 'My admiration and love for the man is boundless. He was a man of vision, compassion and courage, and I only hope the legacy I leave on this earth is as rich and meaningful as his has been.'

Legacies of course can be material as well as spiritual, and news of a sporting auction of Ali's boxing memorabilia was to be held in Los Angeles in October brought a quick reaction from his camp. 'Muhammad wants the public to know that he is not endorsing and not participating in this auction, nor has he provided any items,' said a spokesperson, while the man himself added 'Over the years people around me took things. . . I want all my stuff!'

**Right: 1988. Muhammad Ali and Jack Nicholson.**

when he found A-L-I jumping out of the middle of the word H-E-A-L-I-N-G.

By late 1998, Will Smith's place in the Ali bio-pic seemed to be assured, with Barry Sonnenfeld lined up to direct a film with the title *Power And Grace*. Smith saw his future role as helping him combine elements of comedy, action and drama. 'It would be a combination of Robin Williams, Eddie Murphy and Arnold Schwarzenegger.' And, though it wasn't the first time Ali had appeared to endorse a young actor, an appearance in Smith's video for the hit single 'Just The Two Of Us' with one of his daughters suggested there might be some truth in the rumor.

Also in October, the Muhammad Ali Center in Louisville opened its doors, Governor Patton doing the honors. It had been founded at the second time of asking, and was an attempt by the local boy made good to give something back to the community from which he'd taken on the world — and won. Ironically, just before this new facility bearing his name opened, Ali had sold his training camp to a former aide, George Dillman. He purchased the six-acre site for

**Left: 1986 Olympic Games, Atlanta, Georgia.**

**Below Right: 1996. Sylvester Stallone, Muhammad Ali, Riddick Bowe, Michael Buffer, Sugar Ray Leonard, Lennox Lewis, Vinny Pazienza, and Carl Weathers clench fists at a Rocky anniversary celebration at the All Star Café.**

**Below Left: 29 August, 1996. Ali speaks with First Lady Hillary Clinton, who sits in her box with daughter Chelsea at the 1996 Democratic National Convention.**

**Right: Ali stands next to Evander Holyfield as he speaks at the Muhammad Ali Tribute.**

**Far Right: Ali attends the Mike Tyson hearing, Clark County, Las Vegas.**

but his presence and spirituality. When he came to London in February 1999, fight fans with long memories harked back to June 1963 and his historic Wembley meeting with Henry Cooper, not to mention his two fights within three months in 1966 when first Cooper and then Brian London felt the power of his flailing fists. But three decades and more had passed since then, and people with that kind of recall were thin on the ground. Fans, though, weren't. Amazingly, thousands too young to have seen Ali fight were flocking to touch the hem of his metaphorical garment.

His arrival in Britain in February 1999 was at the behest of Irish rock singer Bono. The frontman of U2 was a big enough name in his own right to hog the headlines, and he was preparing to use the Brits — the British record industry's annual awards show – as his platform. But Bono (real name Paul Hewson) was shrewd enough to realize there was someone he could call upon whose image and resonance spread far beyond even his own.

The cause was a new one, but no less noble than Ali's quest for a cure for Parkinson's. Jubilee 2000, as the campaign was dubbed, was an attempt to get developed nations to cancel Third World debt by the end of the first year of the next millennium. The Pope, the Dalai Lama and Archbishop Desmond Tutu were among Ali's fellow patrons, but only one had graced the occasion with his presence. Muhammad's introduction from the stage led to familiar chants of 'Ali, Ali,' but it was only the following day when he left the company of the music-biz fat cats and took to the streets of London that the real Ali effect was apparent.

The purpose was to visit the Lambeth Refugee Resource and Development Centre, where the Jubilee 2000 campaign was to be opened. This was situated in Brixton, a population center of Londoners of Afro-Caribbean descent, but admirers of every size, color and creed were visible thronging the streets as the champion passed slowly through them in an open-topped Bentley limousine.

Jubilee 2000 director Ann Pettifor explained that Ali's appointment as their international ambassador was because 'He is an icon for all people who have struggled against the inhumanity of racism and war. He carries his scars and his achievements with tremendous dignity.' That dignity, she continued, was 'shared

**Left: The Ali tribute featuring Evander Holyfield.**

by the millions in Africa, Latin America and Asia who daily struggle against the economic, human and social degradation caused by debt.' Certainly Ali's world travels on humanitarian causes had given him first-hand experience of that.

True to the multi-cultural nature of the event, Ali wore a pullover knitted in different colours as he held children in his arms, signed autographs and pressed the flesh. Next came a series of familiar magic tricks as he made a red handkerchief vanish before getting down to business. On arrival at the center, he signed his most important autograph of the day when he added his name to Jubilee 2000's petition. Then he went into closed session with the leaders of the campaign, accompanied by his agent and lawyer Ron DiNicola. Apparently, those who were privileged enough to participate were awed by his presence; when a speaker put across the point that the objective was to bring freedom to the countries shackled by debt, Ali rose to his feet, all eyes upon him... only to silently punch the air with his fist in a victory gesture. The room erupted...

Earlier that day, he had joined half a dozen children to lay wreaths of remembrance at a monument in Westminster, Central London. The children were symbolic of the young lives that could be saved if Third

**Right: 26 September, 1998. Ali deep in thought in Melbourne, Australia.**

World countries could use their money for investment rather than paying off paper debts to the developed world — an estimated seven million lives were at stake by the end of the year 2000. After a one-minute silence, Ron DiNicola expressed Ali's gratitude at his reception in words.

'It's a terrific honor for Muhammad to be in a country he loves and one he's had a warm and long-standing relationship with. He has had a long-standing commitment to the people of Africa and the other poor countries of the world, and it's an honor for him to be here in support of such a worthy cause.'

Those who met Ali were suitably impressed. Campaign co-ordinator Kofi Mawuli Klu said that he had 'lifted our spirits by identifying himself with this campaign because he only fights just causes,' adding that the former champion had already 'changed the world for many black people by what he did in the ring.' Similarly, Toure Moussa Zeguen, who'd fled to Britain from the Ivory Coast, was hopeful Ali's inter-

**Left: September 1997. Evander Holyfield speaks at the Muhammad Ali Tribute.**

vention would bring the campaign closer to its goal. 'It will take the G8 (developed) countries to cancel the debts,' he said after meeting his hero, 'but Ali has made us believe it can happen.'

Though he enjoyed the love and adulation of millions, thanks largely to using his public image for good in the latter half of the 1990s, Muhammad Ali also derived great pleasure from time spent on his farm in Berrien Springs with his nearest and dearest. Washington Post staff writer David Maraniss was offered a rare glimpse of The Greatest on home turf in summer 1997, and reported a man with much more going for him than many had thought.

'His disorder... is not as debilitating as one might suspect from catching a brief glimpse of him,' said Maraniss. 'He is agile enough to dress himself each morning. He knots his ties perfectly. He lifts his legs to put on his socks. Laces his shoes. Slips on his Swiss Army watch. Feeds himself. Opens doors. Performs magic tricks. Reads his Bibles and Korans. Writes

**Right: April 1997. Ali walks with his wife, Lonnie, at the Essence Awards.**

**Far Right Above: 26 September, 1998. Ali in Melbourne, Australia.**

**Far Right Below: 16 January, 1999. Ali sits next to his daughter Leila during the Mike Tyson and Francois Botha fight at the MGM Grand Garden Arena in Las Vegas. Tyson won the fight after a KO in the 5th round.**

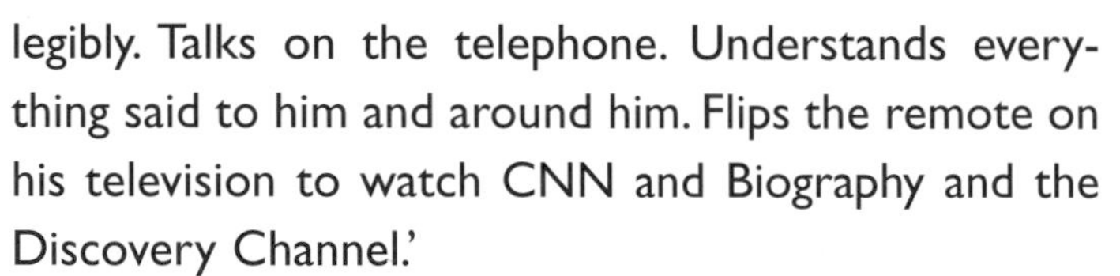

legibly. Talks on the telephone. Understands everything said to him and around him. Flips the remote on his television to watch CNN and Biography and the Discovery Channel.'

A contemplative Ali revealed to Maraniss that he was contemplating his forthcoming 'House in Heaven.' Explaining he could make a 'hundred dollars a picture' signing autographs, he said that, now he wasn't fighting any more, he signed them for nothing. 'Get the money, give it to the homeless ... Give it to soup lines if I see someone who needs some. Here's a hundred. Here's fifty. Soup vendor. Wino. Old woman with varicose veins. Good deeds. . . Whatever colour you are, no matter how much money you have — politics, sports — you're gonna die.' Life, he concluded, was 'A test. Trying to pass the test. I'm trying. . .'

As the millennium approached, Muhammad Ali continued to travel the world, spending an average of 275 days a year on the road meeting presidents, monarchs, religious leaders and the common man. The torch had yet to splutter and die: the flame still burned in the soul of the man they called The Greatest.

**Left: January 1988. Muhammad Ali in the Tournament of Roses Parade.**

**Next Page: 1996. Muhammad Ali receives an honorary gold medal from Samaranch, the President of the International Olympic Committee at the 1996 Olympic Games.**

MUHAMMAD ALI'S

# FIGHT RECORD

USA
USA
OLYMPIC TEAM

# Muhammad Ali's FIGHT RECORD

| DATE | OPPONENT | VENUE | RESULT ROUND | |
|---|---|---|---|---|
| **1960** | | | | |
| 29 OCTOBER | **Tunney Hunsaker** | LOUISVILLE, KENTUCKY | **W** 6 | |
| 27 DECEMBER | **Herb Siler** | MIAMI BEACH, FLORIDA | **W KO** 4 | |
| **1961** | | | | |
| 17 JANUARY | **Tony Esperti** | MIAMI BEACH | **W KO** 3 | |
| 7 FEBRUARY | **Jim Robinson** | MIAMI BEACH | **W KO** 1 | |
| 21 FEBRUARY | **Donnie Fleeman** | MIAMI BEACH | **W KO** 7 | |
| 19 APRIL | **Jim Robinson** | LOUISVILLE | **W KO** 2 | |
| 26 JUNE | **Tony Esperti** | LAS VEGAS, NEVADA | **W** 10 | |
| 22 JULY | **Jim Robinson** | LOUISVILLE | **W** 10 | |
| 7 OCTOBER | **Tony Esperti** | LOUISVILLE | **W KO** 6 | |
| 29 NOVEMBER | **Jim Robinson** | LOUISVILLE | **W KO** 7 | |
| **1962** | | | | |
| 10 FEBRUARY | **Sonny Banks** | NEW YORK | **W KO** 4 | |
| 28 FEBRUARY | **Don Warner** | MIAMI BEACH | **W KO** 4 | |
| 23 APRIL | **George Logan** | LOS ANGELES, CALIFORNIA | **W KO** 4 | |
| 19 MAY | **Billy Daniels** | NEW YORK | **W KO** 7 | |
| 20 JULY | **Alejandro Lavorrante** | LOS ANGELES | **W KO** 5 | |
| 15 NOVEMBER | **Archie Moore** | LOS ANGELES | **W KO** 4 | |
| **1963** | | | | |
| 24 JANUARY | **Charlie Powell** | PITTSBURGH, PENNSYLVANIA | **W KO** 3 | |
| 13 MARCH | **Doug Jones** | NEW YORK | **W KO** 7 | |
| 18 JUNE | **Henry Cooper** | WEMBLEY, LONDON | **W rsf** 5 | |
| **1964** | | | | |
| 25 FEBRUARY | **Sonny Liston** | MIAMI | **W rtd** 7 | WON WORLD HEAVYWEIGHT TITLE |
| **1965** | | | | |
| 25 MAY | **Sonny Liston** | LEWISTON, MAINE | **W KO** 1 | RETAINED WORLD TITLE |
| 22 NOVEMBER | **Floyd Patterson** | LAS VEGAS | **W rsf** 12 | RETAINED WORLD TITLE |

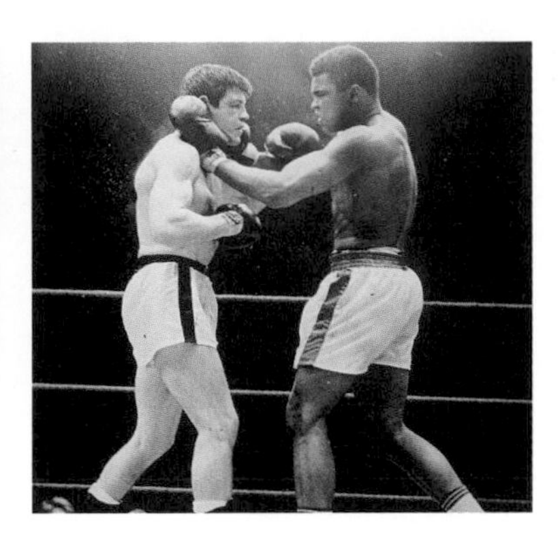

| **1966** | | | | |
|---|---|---|---|---|
| 29 MARCH | **George Chuvalo** | TORONTO, CANADA | **W** 15 | RETAINED WORLD TITLE |
| 21 MAY | **Henry Cooper** | HIGHBURY, LONDON | **W rsf** 6 | RETAINED WORLD TITLE |
| 6 AUGUST | **Brian London** | LONDON | **W KO** 3 | RETAINED WORLD TITLE |
| 10 SEPTEMBER | **Karl Mildenberger** | FRANKFURT, WEST GERMANY | **W KO** 12 | RETAINED WORLD TITLE |
| 14 NOVEMBER | **Cleveland Williams** | HOUSTON, TEXAS | **W KO** 3 | RETAINED WORLD TITLE |
| **1967** | | | | |
| 6 FEBRUARY | **Ernie Terrell** | HOUSTON | **W** 15 | RETAINED WORLD TITLE |
| 22 MARCH | **Zora Folley** | NEW YORK | **W KO** 7 | RETAINED WORLD TITLE |
| | EXILED FROM APRIL 1967 TO SEPTEMBER 1970 AND STRIPPED OF WORLD TITLE | | | |
| **1970** | | | | |
| 26 OCTOBER | **Jerry Quarry** | ATLANTA, GEORGIA | **W rsf** 3 | |
| 7 DECEMBER | **Oscar Bonavena** | NEW YORK | **W KO** 15 | |
| **1971** | | | | |
| 8 MARCH | **Joe Frazier** | NEW YORK | **L** 15 | |
| 26 JULY | **Jimmy Ellis** | HOUSTON | **W KO** 12 | |
| 17 NOVEMBER | **Buster Mathis** | HOUSTON | **W** 10 | |
| 26 DECEMBER | **Jurgen Blin** | ZURICH, SWITZERLAND | **W KO** 7 | |

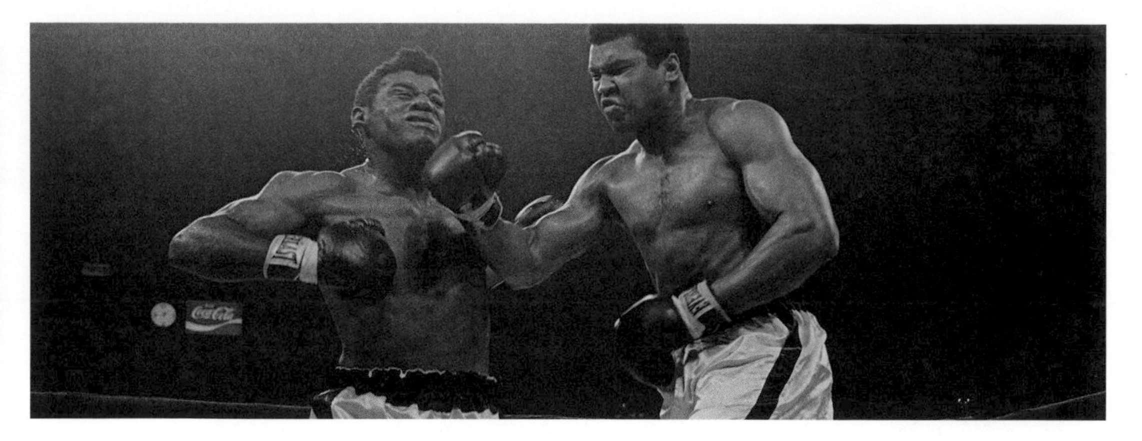

## 1972

| | | | | |
|---|---|---|---|---|
| 1 APRIL | **Mac Foster** | TOKYO | **W** 15 | |
| 1 MAY | **George Chuvalo** | VANCOUVER, CANADA | **W** 12 | |
| 27 JUNE | **Jerry Quarry** | LAS VEGAS | **W rsf** 7 | |
| 19 JULY | **Al 'Blue' Lewis** | DUBLIN, IRELAND | **W KO** 11 | |
| 20 SEPTEMBER | **Floyd Patterson** | NEW YORK | **W rsf** 7 | |
| 21 NOVEMBER | **Bob Foster** | LAKE TAHOE, NEVADA | **W KO** 8 | |

## 1973

| | | | | |
|---|---|---|---|---|
| 14 FEBRUARY | **Joe Bugner** | LAS VEGAS | **W** 12 | |
| 31 MARCH | **Ken Norton** | SAN DIEGO, CALIFORNIA | **L** 12 | |
| 10 SEPTEMBER | **Ken Norton** | LOS ANGELES, CALIFORNIA | **W** 12 | |
| 20 OCTOBER | **Rudi Lubbers** | JAKARTA, INDONESIA | **W** 12 | |

## 1974

| | | | | |
|---|---|---|---|---|
| 28 JANUARY | **Joe Frazier** | NEW YORK | **W** 12 | |
| 30 OCTOBER | **George Foreman** | KINSHASA, ZAIRE | **W KO** 8 | REGAINED WORLD TITLE |

## 1975

| | | | | |
|---|---|---|---|---|
| 24 MARCH | **Chuck Wepner** | CLEVELAND, OHIO | **W KO** 15 | RETAINED WORLD TITLE |
| 16 MAY | **Ron Lyle** | LAS VEGAS | **W KO** 11 | RETAINED WORLD TITLE |
| 30 JUNE | **Joe Bugner** | KUALA LUMPUR, MALAYSIA | **W** 15 | RETAINED WORLD TITLE |
| 30 SEPTEMBER | **Joe Frazier** | MANILA, PHILIPPINES | **W rtd** 14 | RETAINED WORLD TITLE |

## 1976

| | | | | |
|---|---|---|---|---|
| 20 FEBRUARY | **Jean Pierre Coopman** | SAN JUAN, MEXICO | **W KO** 5 | RETAINED WORLD TITLE |
| 30 APRIL | **Jimmy Young** | LANDOVER | **W** 15 | RETAINED WORLD TITLE |
| 24 MAY | **Richard Dunn** | MUNICH, WEST GERMANY | **W KO** 5 | RETAINED WORLD TITLE |
| 28 SEPTEMBER | **Ken Norton** | NEW YORK | **W** 15 | RETAINED WORLD TITLE |

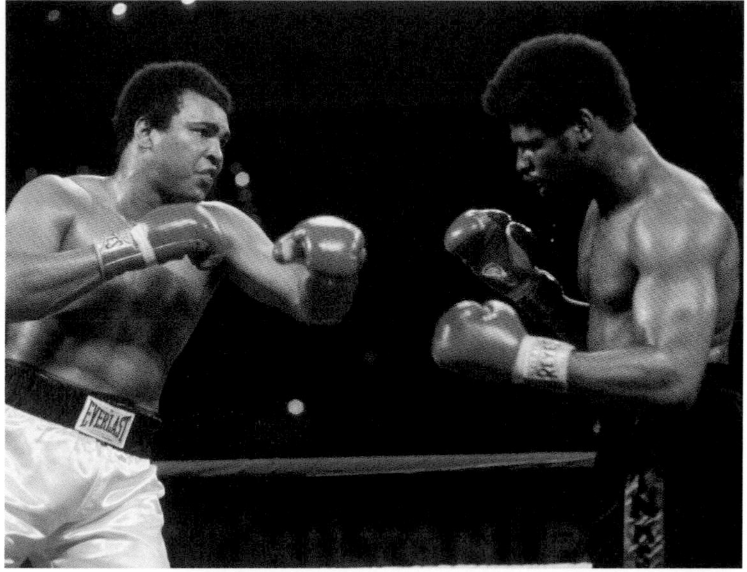

## 1977

| | | | | |
|---|---|---|---|---|
| 16 MAY | **Alfredo Evangelista** | LANDOVER | **W** 15 | RETAINED WORLD TITLE |
| 29 SEPTEMBER | **Earnie Shavers** | NEW YORK | **W** 15 | RETAINED WORLD TITLE |

## 1978

| | | | | |
|---|---|---|---|---|
| 15 FEBRUARY | **Leon Spinks** | LAS VEGAS | **L** 15 | LOST WORLD TITLE |
| 15 SEPTEMBER | **Leon Spinks** | NEW ORLEANS, LOUISIANA | **W** 15 | REGAINED WORLD TITLE |

## 1979

ANNOUNCED RETIREMENT

## 1980

| | | | | |
|---|---|---|---|---|
| 2 OCTOBER | **Larry Holmes** | LAS VEGAS | **L rtd** 11 | FOR WORLD TITLE |

## 1981

| | | | | |
|---|---|---|---|---|
| 11 DECEMBER | **Trevor Berbick** | NASSAU, BAHAMAS | **L** 10 | |

# INDEX



**Left: 1980, Las Vegas. Muhammadi Ali vs. Larry Holmes, Press Conference.**

# CREDITS

**ACKNOWLEDGEMENTS**

The publisher wishes to thank all the picture libraries and photographers who supplied the illustrations for this book. The photographs on the following pages were kindly provided by:

Corbis/Bettmann for pages 2, 10, 11, 12, 14, 16, 19, 20, 22-23, 24-25, 27, 28-29, 31, 32, 33, 34-35, 38-39, 40, 41, 42-43, 45, 46 (both), 47, 51, 52, 53, 54, 55, 56, 57, 58-59 (both), 60-61 (both), 65, 66, 67, 68, 69-70 (both), 72, 73, 74, 76-77, 79, 80, 81, 84-85, 86-87, 88, 89 (right), 92-93, 94-95, 96-97, 104-105 (both), 106-107 (both), 109 (both), 112, 113, 114-115, 116-117, 118, 119, 121, 122 (all), 125 (bottom), 128-129, 130, 131, 132, 133, 136, 138, 139, 154, 155 (left and middle), 156 (both) and 157 (both)

Allsport/MSI for pages 7, 13, 63 (bottom), 75, 82-83 and 100

Corbis/Charles Harris; Pittsburgh Courier for pages 8-9 and 37

Allsport for pages 15, 91, 99, 120 and 123

Corbis/Hulton-Deutsch Collection for front cover and pages 17 and 48-49

Allsport/Hulton Deutsch for pages 50, 62, 63 (top), 64, 89 (left), 108 and 155 (right)

Corbis/Jerry Cooke for page 98

Corbis/Michael Brennan for back cover and pages 101, 102, 111, 124, 125 (top left and right), 145 (all), 146 (left), 149 and 150 (bottom right)

Allsport/Tony Duffy for page 103

Allsport/Steve Powell for pages 127 (all) and 159

Corbis/David Rubinger for page 134

Corbis/Joseph Sohm; ChromoSohm, Inc. for page 135

Allsport/Gray Mortimore for page 137

Corbis for page 141 (top)

Corbis/Lynn Goldsmith for pages 141 (bottom) and 142

Allsport/Michael Cooper for page 143 (top)

Corbis/Wally McNamee for page 143 (bottom left)

Corbis/Mitchell Gerber for pages 143 (bottom right), 144 (both) and 150 (left)

Allsport/Harry How for page 146 (right)

Allsport/Andy Lyons for page 147

Allsport Australia/Jack Atley for pages 148 and 150 (top right)

Corbis/Neil Rabinowitz for page 151

Corbis/Ales Fevzer for pages 153